Mrs. John King Van Rensselaer

The devil's picture-books

A history of playing cards

Mrs. John King Van Rensselaer

The devil's picture-books
A history of playing cards

ISBN/EAN: 9783741133633

Manufactured in Europe, USA, Canada, Australia, Japa

Cover: Foto ©Andreas Hilbeck / pixelio.de

Manufactured and distributed by brebook publishing software (www.brebook.com)

Mrs. John King Van Rensselaer

The devil's picture-books

Plate 1.

THE

DEVIL'S PICTURE-BOOKS

A History of Playing-Cards

BY

MRS. JOHN KING VAN RENSSELAER
AUTHOR OF CROCHET LACE, ETC.

ILLUSTRATED

NEW YORK
DODD, MEAD, AND COMPANY
PUBLISHERS

PREFACE.

THE "Devil's Books" was the name bestowed upon Playing-cards by the Puritans and other pious souls who were probably in hopes that this name would alarm timid persons and so prevent their use. Whether or not his Satanic Majesty originated Playing-cards, we have no means of discovering; but it is more probable that he only inspired their invention, and placed them in the hands of mankind, who have eagerly adopted this simple means of amusing themselves, and have used it according to the good or evil which predominated in their own breasts. Many learned men have written books or treatises on Playing-cards, and I am indebted for a large part of the information contained in this history to "Les Cartes à Jouer," by M. Paul la Croix; "Facts and Speculations about Playing-cards," by Mr. Chatto; "The History of Playing-cards," by the Rev. Edward Taylor; and "The History of Playing-cards," by Mr. Singer.

These books are now out of print, and somewhat difficult to obtain; and I hope, by bringing into a small compass the principal features set forth in them, I shall be able to place before a number of readers interesting facts that would be otherwise unobtainable.

Hearty thanks are due to the custodians of the National Museum in Washington, who have aided me in every way in their power, and also to the many kind friends who have sought far and wide for unique and uncommon packs of cards, and helped materially by gathering facts relating to them for me.

That many nations have cards peculiar to their own country and almost unknown beyond its boundaries may be a matter of surprise to some; that such ordinary and familiar objects as Playing-cards should have a history, will astonish others. My hope is that the subject will interest my readers as it has done me. Any facts concerning Playing-cards or any communications relating to rare or curious packs will be gladly received by the author, who would like to add to her collection.

M. K. VAN RENSSELAER.

NEW YORK, 1890.

CONTENTS.

	PAGE
THE TAROTS, OR THE FIRST CARDS	11
CHESS	21
ENGRAVING	33
MATERIALS	41
NAME	49
CLASSIFICATION OF PACKS OF CARDS INTO SUITS	55
CARDS OF DIFFERENT COUNTRIES, VIZ.:—	
CHINA	65
EGYPT	69
INDIA	70
CASHMERE	74
PERSIA	77
ITALY	80
GERMANY	83
SPAIN	88
FRANCE	90
ENGLAND	102
AMERICA	112
JAPAN	131
THE KING	139
THE QUEEN	151
THE KNAVE	161
ACES AND OTHER CARDS	171
USE AND ABUSE	179
PIPS, SUITS, AND COLOURS	191
ODDS AND ENDS	201

LIST OF ILLUSTRATIONS.

	PLATE
PERSIAN	1
TAROT	2
TAROT	3
CHINESE	4
CASHMERE. Cards owned by Lockwood de Forest, Esq.	5, 6
ITALIAN CARDS SHOWING THE SUITS OF SWORDS, MACES, MONEY, AND CUPS. Owned by Mrs. J. K. Van Rensselaer	7
GERMAN CARDS SHOWING THE ACES OF GRÜN, ROTH, SCHELLEN, AND HERZEN. Owned by Mrs. J. K. Van Rensselaer	8
REMAINS OF THE PACK SUPPOSED TO HAVE BEEN USED BY CHARLES VII. OF FRANCE, DATE 1425. In the Cabinet des Estampes, Paris, France	9
ELIZABETH OF YORK	10
CARDS FOUND BY MR. CHATTO IN A BLACK-LETTER VOLUME FORMERLY IN THE CATHEDRAL LIBRARY, AT PETERBOROUGH, ENGLAND. Now in the Print Room of the British Museum	11
FOUND IN AN OLD EDITION OF CLAUDIAN, EARLY ENGLISH	12
CARDS ON WHICH INVITATIONS WERE WRITTEN. Owned by Mrs. Ten Eyck and Miss Crowninshield. Date 1763	13

viii *List of Illustrations.*

PLATE

GEOGRAPHICAL CARDS, Owned by Richard H. Derby, Esq.,
M.D. Date 1795 14

NORTH AMERICAN INDIAN CARDS, APACHE TRIBE. Cut out
of Deerskin and painted by themselves. National Museum,
Washington, D. C., U. S. A. 15, 16, 17

NORTH AMERICAN INDIAN GAMBLING-STICKS, HAIDA TRIBE,
QUEEN CHARLOTTE ISLANDS. Carved on Cubes of Wood.
National Museum, Washington, D. C., U. S. A. . . . 18, 19

NORTH AMERICAN INDIAN GAMBLING-STICKS, ALASKA TRIBE.
Painted on Cubes of Wood. National Museum, Washington, D. C., U. S. A. 20

JAPANESE CARDS, EACH ONE REPRESENTING A WEEK IN THE
YEAR. Owned by Mrs. J. K. Van Rensselaer . . 21, 22, 23, 24

THE DEVIL'S PICTURE-BOOKS

*"The Ladies arm-in-arm in clusters,
As great and gracious a' as sisters;
. . . . .
On lee-lang nights, wi' crabbit leuks,
Pore owre the devil's pictured beuks."*

BURNS.

THE TAROTS.

THE DEVIL'S PICTURE-BOOKS.

THE TAROTS.

A youth of frolic, an old age of cards.
   HONE: *Every-Day Book*, ii. 98.

THE origin of Playing-cards and their inventor is still a subject of speculation, and will probably remain forever undiscovered. Almost every country in Europe has through her scholars laid claim to having been the first to use cards; and many documentary and other proofs have been brought forward to substantiate their assertions, which are based upon ancient laws, common traditions, or contemporary illustrations.

That cards were brought from the East to Europe about the time of the Crusades, and probably by the home-returning warriors, who imported many of the newly acquired customs and habits of the Orient into their own countries, seems to be a well established fact; and it does not contradict the statement made by some writers, who declare that the gypsies — who about that time began to wander over Europe — brought with them and introduced cards, which they used, as they do at the present day, for divining the future. Cards may well have become known by both means, and they spread rapidly over all of what was then considered the only civilized part of the world; and the proofs that have been brought forward show that they were known nearly simultaneously in Italy, Spain, France, Germany, and England, and point to a common origin not to be found in any one of these countries.

The first cards known in Europe, and which were named *Tarots, Tarocchi*, etc., seem to differ in almost every respect from those of the fifteenth century, although these probably inspired their invention. The latter resemble much more those of the present day than they do the original Tarots. The first packs consisted of seventy-eight cards, — that is, of four suits of numeral cards; and besides these there were twenty-two emblematical pictured cards, which were called *Atous*,

Plate 2.

or *Atouts*, — a word which M. Duchesne, a French writer, declares signifies "above all." This word used in French has the same meaning as our word *Trump*. The marks which distinguish the Tarot suits are usually *Swords*, *Cups*, *Sticks*, and *Money*; and each one consists of fourteen cards, ten of which are "pips" and three or four "coat" cards, — namely, King, Queen, Knight, and Knave. The Queen was not always admitted. These suits seem to be the origin of the modern packs; and the emblems used on them have been adopted in many countries where the *Atout* part was discarded while the rest of the pack with its original symbols was retained.

Mr. Singer gives a graphic description of these cards and the games to be played with them, and says that "among different nations the suits [as will be hereafter shown] are distinguished by marks peculiar to themselves, while only the general features of the numbered cards headed by figures or court cards have been retained."

The second division of the Tarot pack, called *Atouts*, are numbered up to twenty-one, each of these having its proper value; and besides all these there is one, not numbered and not belonging to the division of the suit cards, which is called a *Fou*, and in playing the game is designated *Mat*, or *il Matto*. This " Joker," as we should term it, has no value of its own, but augments that of any of the Atouts to which it may be joined, and is sometimes played instead of a Queen, being then called " her Excuse."

These Atouts are each represented by a print which is supposed to resemble some character, and the name is generally placed on the card. Among them are an Emperor, a Cupid, a Chariot, a Hermit, a Gallows, Death, The Day of Judgment, a Pope, Fortune, Temperance, Justice, the Moon, the Sun, etc. The order in which they are placed is not always the same, and is seemingly unimportant. The game may be played by two or four persons. " The one who holds the ' Fool ' regains his stake; ' La Force ' (or Strength) takes twice as much from the pool, while ' La Mort ' (or Death) most appropriately sweeps the board."

It is said that the distribution of the suit cards has a peculiar signification. Each one is distinguished by an emblem which represents the four classes into which communities were once divided. First comes the Churchman, represented by the

Chalice (or Copas); next in rank, the Warrior, whose emblem is the Sword; third, the Merchant, symbolized by a Coin; and fourth, the Workman with his Staff. It will be shown hereafter that almost all writers on the subject allow the possibility of the divisions of the suits being shown in the cards.

The earliest known specimens of these Tarot cards are now to be found in the Cabinet des Estampes in Paris, and are supposed to have formed part of the pack which was painted for King Charles the Seventh of France in 1393, to cheer and amuse him during an illness which had been caused by a *coup-de-soleil* in 1392, and which made him a melancholy but not a dangerous lunatic. M. Paul la Croix describes these Tarots as having been most delicately painted and resembling in treatment the illuminations of manuscripts. They are on a golden background on which dots forming an ornamental pattern were impressed. A border of silver surrounded and as it were framed each picture, through which a dotted line twisted spirally like a ribbon. M. la Croix points out that this dotted line, in his language technically termed a *tare* (which also means a "fault" or "defect"), was a sort of fluting produced by small holes pricked into the substance of which the cards were made, and fancies that to these Tares the Tarots owe their name. Other writers, however, dispute this derivation of the word, and discover new ones for themselves which are generally quite as fanciful and far-fetched.

These well preserved Tarots are eighteen centimetres by nine, and are painted in water colours on a thin card. The composition of the figures is ingenious and artistic. The drawing is correct and full of character, and the colours are still brilliant. A narrow border of black and white checks surrounds each one. This border is a piece of checkered paper pasted on the back of the card and neatly folded over its edge as if to protect it, showing on the face of the card and forming a frame for the pictures. This fashion of having a checkered or diapered back was closely followed in many of the countries where cards have been used; and these backs are still seen, although this old pattern (which, as will hereafter be seen, had probably a very interesting origin) has been generally discarded, and each card-maker

Plate 3.

The Tarots.

adopts a different device with which to decorate the backs of his cards according to his own fancy. In France the backs are generally plain, and coloured red, pink, or blue. In Spain the pattern is dotted on the surface in lines and circles, while in other countries interlaced and meaningless designs are employed.

Packs of cards closely resembling the original Tarots are still to be found in some parts of Switzerland, Germany, and Alsace, where they are used by the peasantry in the districts which are not much frequented by travellers; but they are unknown to the rest of the world except as curiosities. They are, however, the sole representatives of the cards which the Crusaders or the gypsies brought into Europe, and which the latter use whenever possible to divine the future or recall the past. Some writers point to the eastern origin of these Tarots, because in them "Death" is numbered thirteen, and the idea of fatality or bad luck attached to that number is essentially Oriental; and they declare that the fact that the emblematical Atouts are numbered from low to high, just as certain Asiatic alphabets are written from left to right, may cover a similar interpretation.

CHESS.

CHESS.

ALMOST all writers on Cards have admitted the strong resemblance they bear to Chess; and M. Paul la Croix declares that in comparatively modern times the game of chess and games of cards showed strikingly similar features, which demonstrated their common origin,—the art of painting being resorted to to depict the one, and that of sculpture to represent the other.

A pretty history of the origin of Chess has been related. It states that the game was invented for the amusement of an Oriental potentate, and was played with living figures, who were required to move at the word of command from one square to another of a huge tiled court-yard which was surrounded by the balconies of the palace and its harem, from which all the movements of the pieces on the pavement below could be watched by the sovereign and his court. Living games of Chess have been played for amusement or "sweet charity's sake" even in modern times; but such cumbersome pieces must have been difficult to manage, and it was only natural that the ingenious mind which contrived living chessmen should soon have superseded them with figures carved in a convenient material such as wood or ivory, and then placed the mimic armies on a miniature battle-field which could be easily commanded by two or more players.

The Eastern origin of Chess is undisputed, but when and by whom it was introduced into Europe is unknown. According to Herodius, the Lydians suffered from a long and severe famine in the reign of Atys, and in order to forget their misery, invented many games, particularly dice. Previous writers attribute the invention of games of chance to the Greeks during the siege of Troy, and Cicero mentions *games* in the camp; but it does not follow that these games were either chess, cards, or dice. They may have been knuckle-bones or jack-stones, as that game was known in very early days, and pictures representing persons playing with them have been found among Egyptian antiquities.

It has been asserted positively by the oldest traditions that the cards of Indian origin are only chessmen transferred to paper on which the principal pieces of the game are reproduced, the game being improved by admitting more than two players.

In the game of Chess there are generally only two armies of pawns, each one being commanded by a King, a Vizir (which in the lapse of years has become a Queen), a Knight, an Elephant (which became a fool and after that a Bishop), and a Dromedary (afterward a Castle); and the game shows a striking similarity to the Indian games of cards, which have eight companies distinguished by their colours and emblems, and of which each one has their King, their Vizir, and their Elephant. The two games differ, of course; but sufficient resemblances between them remain to show their common origin, which recalls the terrible game of war, in which each adversary must assault, manœuvre, make combinations, and exert eternal vigilance.

We learn from a most reliable source (Abel de Rémusat, Journal asiatique, September, 1822) that playing-cards came to Europe from India and

China, and that, like the game of Chess, they were known to the Arabians and the Saracens from the beginning of the twelfth century. At first these games found little popular favour, most probably because they were introduced at a period when civil and ecclesiastical authorities most positively forbade all games of chance.

From India Chess spread gradually to other countries. The Persians seem to have known it about the middle of the sixth century; and Singer, in his "History of Playing-cards," states that it reached China at nearly the same period, and in the reign of the Emperor Wa-si.

There are such striking resemblances between the figures used in Chess and those on cards as to leave very little doubt where the inspiration for the latter originated.

Beautiful circular cards made of ivory have been found, on which the figures are painted as if the artist were unable to carve the forms that he desired to represent, and therefore was obliged to paint them on a flat surface. These cards are small disks, which might easily be placed on the squares of a board and moved from one to the other like chessmen. The advantage of commanding a concealed army instead of one spread out on an open field probably soon became apparent, and the result was that some slight changes in the shape of the pictured figure and the material used were soon made, which with various modifications have come down to us as the modern playing-card.

If a study is made of some of the different packs of Chinese cards, it will be seen that horses, deer, and other animals are represented on them, together with symbols which seem to mark the suits. In other packs, instead of the figure of the animal, Chinese characters are placed above the symbol marking the suit, which characters seem to have been put there instead of the picture, and which it is affirmed state, " This is the horse," or " This one is the deer," as the case may be, — as if on one of our court cards the legend " This is the Queen " should be written on its face, instead of placing there the quaintly garbed female form which usually represents that august person.

We find the principal figures from the chessboard reproduced in the Tarots, and also in some of the Spanish and German packs. There is the

King, the Knight, or mounted horseman, and the Knave. The pawns or common soldiers are represented by numbers; but there is this difference between Cards and the game of Chess as it is generally played,—in the former there are four armies, or as we should call them "suits," and each one is headed by the King instead of the two sides generally seen in Chess. Now, Mr. Chatto remarks that there is an Indian game of Chess which is called *Chaturanga*, or "The Four Kings," in which two allied armies play against the same opponents. He also gives a few rules for this game. "Having marked eight squares on all sides," says the Sage, "place the *red* army to the east, the *green* to the south, the *yellow* to the west, and the *black* to the north." It is worthy of notice that these colours form the ground of four of the suits of one of the divisions of an eight-suit pack of Hindostanee cards; and this supports the theory that the painted ivory disks might have originally been used on the chessboard and then held in the hand. This strange Indian game of Chess would also point to the first division of the mimic warriors into four armies, each one distinguished by its uniform of different colours, which when placed in the cards became known as "suits." This word was probably derived from the French *en suite*, which signifies "to follow."

There is another game known in which two chess-boards are joined. "It is played by two persons on each side, each of whom is concerned to defend his own game at the same time that he co-operates with his ally to distress by every means in his power the two armies opposed to them." "Four-handed Chess" is described in Hoyle's Book of Games, which illustrates a board with one hundred and sixty squares. The game is played with four sets of chessmen, coloured, respectively, white, black, red, and green, like those of the Indian game.

The Queen, both in Chess and Cards, has a European if not an entirely French origin. She takes the place of the Eastern Vizir, or General; and it may be particularly remarked that in the game of Chess she is more of an Amazon or Joan of Arc than the consort of a reigning monarch. Her height also is excessive for a woman, in proportion to the other pieces, and her active duties of harassing the enemy and protecting her slow-moving husband while leading his army to battle show that although she is called a Queen she is usurping the position of a general, who could more appropriately fill this important, active, and warlike place than she can.

In the Card Kingdom the Queen is a much more lifelike and womanly person, as in it she aids and abets her sovereign lord and master, and is generally meekly subordinate to him.

While drawing attention to the resemblances between the games of Chess and of Cards, we must not forget to notice a slight but perhaps important fact; and that is that all the ancient packs had *checkered* backs, as if the little army were loath to leave the old battle-field, but transferred it to their backs, and exposed that to the gaze of the opponent instead of standing in battle-array upon it. The oldest existing packs or Tarots retain these checkered backs; and some authors have decided that *Tarot* means "checkered," and that the name is derived from this circumstance.

The author of "Playing and Other Cards in the British Museum," Mr. W. H. Wiltshire, derides the idea that cards derive their origin from the chessmen, and points out the fact that "in all such games there are certain approximations, although hardly enough to establish an identity of origin. Chess," he says, "is a game of calculation and combinations; cards are purely chance." This seems hardly a fair objection, as there are many games of cards that call for calculations and combinations, some of them requiring much thought and study, although on the other hand there are many that may be played mechanically and without bestowing much thought upon them. Mr. Wiltshire also declares "that in Chess the pieces are exposed and the positions equalized, while the cards are hidden, and the cleverest person may be beaten by a novice without having made one trick." Some particular game of cards may have been in the author's mind when he made this statement; but there are a great many card games about which it would not be true.

ENGRAVING.

ENGRAVING.

THE order obtained in 1441 by the master card-makers of Venice from their Senate which prohibited the introduction into that city of "large quantities of cards printed and painted outside of Venice," should be particularly noticed, as printed cards are especially mentioned as well as painted ones; and this points to the fact that there was in use some process besides the original one of painting or stencilling when the cards of that period were being manufactured.

The fragments of the French packs which show by many marks but particularly by their costumes that they were executed about the time of Charles the Seventh, were possibly some of the first efforts of the wood-engraver. They were probably produced between the years 1420 and 1440, — that is, before the greater part of the xylographies now known.

The first pictures produced by printing with blocks of wood were probably used as playing-cards; and this is an invention which is very much older than that of printing with movable types.

By the middle of the fifteenth century cards had spread all over Europe, and necessity called for an economical process by which they might be rapidly as well as cheaply produced.

In 1392 three packs of Tarots were painted for the King of France by Jacquemin Gringonneur, for which he received fifty-six sols parisis, — that is to say, about one hundred and seventy francs, or thirty-four dollars.

A single pack of Tarots, which were charmingly painted about 1415 by Marziano, Secretary to the Duc de Milan, cost fifteen thousand écus d'or (about five hundred dollars); and in 1454 a pack of cards intended for a dauphin of France cost only fourteen or fifteen francs, or three dollars. In the thirty years which had elapsed it is evident that a cheap process of manufacturing cards had been discovered.

Cards had also become merchandise, and were sold at the same time as counters, or *épingles;* and from the latter is derived the French expression "tirer son épingle de jeu."

Engraving. 35

It has generally been conceded that the Chinese understood the art of wood-engraving long before it was practised in Europe. Marco Polo, who visited China about the middle of the thirteenth century, describes, in his interesting book of travels, a mode of printing or stamping with coloured ink; and it is probable that printing from a block was also known to the Chinese at that time.

Authorities do not agree about which are the first specimens of wood-engraving, but it is more than probable that a rude picture of Saint Christopher carrying the infant Jesus, which is dated 1425, is one of the earliest specimens of the art. This curious and interesting print was discovered pasted in the cover of a manuscript in the library of the Chartreuse at Buxheim in Suabia. Mr. Singer gives a description of the infancy of the xylographic art, and says that the demand for playing-cards increased so rapidly after their introduction into the European countries that it became imperative to manufacture them at a moderate price; and thus wood-engraving became of consequence, and its productions soon became a most important article of commerce.

It is probable that at first the wood-engravers

produced only small pictures of saints, influenced no doubt by their priestly surroundings, as nearly all of the early wood-cuts which have been found are of pious subjects; and they were probably executed by the inhabitants of the religious houses, who were at the time the educated men of the day. These early engravings are printed on paper of the shape, size, and style of the earliest known playing-cards. The saints' pictures always bore a small streamer or ribbon, on which the name of the holy person represented was written. On the early specimens of playing-cards names are always placed beside the heads of the court cards; and this may have been necessary in order to distinguish the saint from the king, as it is possible that the engraver may have used the same figures to represent not only the holy personages, but also the members of the royal card family, and they could be distinguished only by the names written beside them.

An old chronicler of the city of Ulm, of about the year 1397, states that playing-cards have been sent in bundles to Italy, Sicily, and other southern countries in exchange for groceries and other merchandise; and it may have been this exportation

Engraving. 37

of cards from Germany, which probably increased most rapidly, that called for the edict forbidding the importation of cards into Venice in 1441. It also points to their having been manufactured in quantities even before 1423, the date of the earliest known wood-cut.

Cards were not only produced by hand-painting, stencilling, or wood-engraving, but really artistic and beautifully executed cards were engraved on copper, in 1466, by an artist known as Le Maître (the Master), but by no other name.

Only a few specimens of these unique cards are now to be found in some museums, and the series is not complete. According to calculation, they should consist of seventy cards, containing five suits instead of four, with fourteen cards in each suit and four figures or court cards to each one. The face cards are the King, Queen, Knight, and Knave; and the marks show a bizarre collection of savages, wild beasts, birds of prey, and flowers. They are grouped and numbered and arranged in such a way as to be easily distinguished and sorted into the correct suits.

In 1463 the card-makers of England endeavoured to protect themselves from the foreign importation of cards, and they must have been a somewhat influential guild even at that early date to require and receive this protection from the Government; but no cards have been discovered that were undoubtedly of English manufacture of that period.

MATERIALS.

MATERIALS.

THE process of manufacturing Playing-cards now deserves attention. It seems that the first packs of Tarots which have been preserved were made of two pieces of card-board, and were afterward pasted together. The backs had a checkered pattern designed on them, and were placed so as to overlap the face; and the diapered edge was carefully pasted down and formed a protection and a frame to the pictured side.

It may be as well to quote here the graphic account given by Mr. Chatto in his "Facts and Speculations on Playing-cards." He says:—

"The following account of the manner of making cards at the manufactory of Messrs. de la Rue & Co. of London is extracted from Bradshaw's Journal, April 16, 1842:—

"'The first object that engages our attention is the preparation of the paper intended to be formed into cards. It is found that ordinary paper when submitted to pressure acquires a certain degree of polish, but not sufficient for playing-cards of the finest quality. In order, therefore, that it may admit of the high finish which is afterwards imparted, the paper is prepared by a white enamel colour consisting of animal size and other compounds. This substance, which renders the paper impermeable to the atmosphere, is laid on with a large brush and left to dry.

"'The paper being ready for use, we proceed to explain the printing of the fronts of the cards, which are technically distinguished as *pips* and *têtes*.

"'To commence with the simpler, the pip (that is, the Hearts, Diamonds, Spades, and Clubs), sets of blocks are produced, each containing forty engravings of one card; and as the ordinary method of letterpress printing is employed, forty impressions of one card are obtained at the same moment. As the pips bear but one colour, black or red, they are worked together at the hand-press or steam-printing machine.

"'For the têtes, however (or court cards), which with the outline contain five colours,—dark blue, light blue, black, red, and yellow,— a somewhat different contrivance is employed. The colours are printed separately, and are made to fit into each other with great nicety, in the same manner as in printing silks or paper-hangings. For this purpose a series of blocks are provided which if united would form the figure intended to be produced. By printing successively from these blocks, the different colours fall into their proper places until the whole process is completed. After the printing is done the sheets are carried into a drying-room heated to 80° Fahrenheit, and are allowed to remain there three or four days, in order to fix the colours.'"

In France the card generally consists of two pieces of paper, but in England a more substantial article is required. It is generally four sheets thick, — that is, the foreside and the back, and two inside layers of an inferior description. The pasting of these sheets together requires care and clever manipulation. After the sheets are pasted together, they are thoroughly dried, enamelled, and then cut into cards which are sorted by being laid out on a table about two hundred at a time, until all the cards that constitute a pack are spread out; so that by this operation two hundred packs are completed almost simultaneously. The best cards are called Moguls; the others, Harrys and Highlanders.

Paper was almost a necessity in card-making; and England could not have provided it when cards were first made there, as the art of paper-making was unknown before the reign of Henry the Seventh, who lived from 1485 to 1509. Even as late as the days of Queen Anne, paper was imported from Germany for the purpose.

Many other materials have been used in manufacturing cards besides paper. As has been mentioned, beautiful packs have been painted on ivory or mother of pearl. Parchment and leather have been often used; thin tablets of wood and large leaves have been pressed into service, as well as stout paper which was neither card nor pasteboard. The Chinese and Hindoos sometimes used a cotton paper so stout and smooth as to make it most suitable for the purpose; and the curious wooden sticks carved with distinguishing figures used by the Haida Indians show perhaps the most peculiar materials used in the manufacture of games.

Mr. Chatto mentions a pack of Hindostanee

cards in the Museum of the Royal Asiatic Society which are made of canvas, and are said to be a thousand years old. He says: " On first handling them they seem to be made of thin veneers of wood. These cards are circular; and the figures or marks appear to be executed by hand, not printed nor stencilled."

The Malays use cards made of cocoanut or palm-tree leaves, which are first well dried, and the symbols or distinctive characters are then traced on the leaf with an iron style.

A story in the " History of the Conquest of Florida," by Garcilasso de la Vega, relates that " the soldiers who were engaged in that expedition, having burnt all their cards after the battle of Manoila (about 1542), made themselves new ones of parchment, which they painted admirably as if they had followed the business all their lives; but as they either could not or would not make so many as were wanted, players had the cards in turn for a limited time."

Such fragile and thin materials have sometimes been used in the production of cards that dealing was difficult and shuffling impossible. One very beautiful pack has been produced, and is preserved in the South Kensington Museum in London, which was embroidered on silk.

Such materials as gold, silver, and tortoise-shell, and even small tiles have been used in the manufacture of cards; but when made from these materials they have been difficult to handle, and have been regarded only as curiosities; and at the present day thick pasteboard, either highly enamelled or quite without glaze of any kind, is in general use all over the world.

NAME.

NAME.

THE first positive mention of Playing-cards is in a manuscript by Nicholas de Covellezzo, which is preserved among the Archives of Viterbo. "In 1379," says the Chronicler, "playing-cards were introduced in Viterbo. These came from the country of the Saracens, and were called *Naïb*." The Italians have for centuries called their cards *Naibi*, and in Spain they are still named *Naypes*.

M. la Croix remarks that in Arabic the word *Naïb* signifies "captain," and declares that this name proves the military origin of Cards, and points to their connection with Chess.

Mr. Taylor, in his work on Playing-cards, quotes from the above-mentioned manuscript by Nicholas de Covellezzo, which records the introduction of cards into Italy, and says: "The use of the term *Naïb* in Italy for cards is one of the strongest proofs of their introduction into Europe by the gypsies. To this day they are called in

Spain *Naypes*, which is clearly a corruption of the Arabic *Nabi*, 'a prophet;' and we have therefore the significant fact that cards have been and are still called in Spain by a title which fortune-tellers (gypsies, in fact) might easily be supposed to claim."

Mr. Singer quotes from various authorities to show the derivation of the word *Naipes*, and says that "it may mean 'flat' or 'even,'" which would describe a card; and also that the Hebrew word *Naibes* denotes "sorcery, fortune-telling, prediction," etc.

Mr. Chatto derives the same word from one found in Hindostanee, *Na-eeb* or *Naib*, which signifies a viceroy, lieutenant, or deputy, and says: "As the game of Chess was known in Hindostan by the name of 'The Four Kings,' if cards were suggested by Chess and invented in the same country, the supposition that they might have been called *Chatier-Nawaub*, 'The Four Viceroys,' as the cognate game of Chess was called 'The Four Kings,' and that this name subsequently became changed into *Chartati-Naib*, is at least as probable as the derivation of *Naipes* from *N. P.*, the initials of Nicolas Pepin, their supposed inventor;" which derivation is gravely given by another author.

It is only in Italy that the old name of *Naipes* or *Naibi* is retained. In Portugal the word has become corrupted into *Naipe;* in Spain, *Naypes* or *Naipes.* In France cards are called *Cartes à jouer;* and a pack is named a *Jeu.* In Germany they are termed *Briefe* and *Karten* and *Spielkarten.* In Holland the name is *Kaarten* or *Speelkaarten;* in Denmark, *Kort* or *Spelkort*; and in Russia, *Kartu.* The term *Alea*, which was frequently employed in ancient ordinances and laws, seems to cover all games of chance, and is not used to signify playing-cards alone. The derivation of the English word *card* from the French *carte* is too plain to require further comment.

THE CLASSIFICATION OF PACKS OF CARDS INTO SUITS.

THE CLASSIFICATION OF PACKS OF CARDS INTO SUITS.

EVER since the fifteenth century evidences of the existence and popularity of cards have been found in Italy, Spain, Germany, and France.

The names, colours, emblems, number, and form change with the countries or caprices of the cardmakers; but what are termed *Cartes Tarots* or *Cartes Françaises* are always the original cards which came from the East, and which are in a greater or less degree faithful imitations of the still more ancient game of Chess.

It is related that on the 5th of March, 1423, Saint Bernardin, of Sienna, addressed a crowd which had assembled before a church in that place, and inveighed with such energy and eloquence against all games of chance that his hearers rushed to search for their dice, their chess, and their cards, and lighting a large bonfire, immolated them on the spot.

One man stood by who watched mournfully the movements of the frantic crowd, and then bursting into tears cried out to the preacher: "Father," quoth he, "I make cards. I have no other work by which I can make a livelihood; by stopping my profession, you condemn me to starve."

"If painting is the only thing you can do for a living," replied the preacher, "take this picture [showing him the sacred monogram surrounded by brilliant rays] and copy it."

The workman followed this advice, and became wealthy by reproducing it.

This tale shows how well established the use of cards was in the fifteenth century; and specimens of the cards of that period are still in existence, and at once strike the observing student with the fact that the four great divisions or suits exist (although with different symbols) in almost all the known packs.

It is probable that in France the Tarots were used for many years exactly as they were when first introduced into that country, until the rearrangement of the pack by the French courtiers for the convenience of their demented sovereign.

When this ingenious condensation of the original pack took place, the symbols of the Orient were discarded, and the adapter chose two colours to represent the different suits, and placed *les Cœurs* (Hearts), *les Carreaux* (Diamonds), *les Piques* (Spades), *les Trifles* (Clubs), as the symbols that marked them instead of those on the Tarots, which were *Denari* (Money), *Spade* (Swords), *Coppe* (Cups), and *Bastoni* (Maces). These devices were not distinguished by particular colours; and it is only when the French cards have been copied and adapted that we find the distinctive colours *red* and *black* marking the divisions of the suits.

Playing-cards without doubt reached Germany through Italy, but during their journey toward the north they lost their Eastern character and their Saracenic name almost at once. They never seem to have been called *Naïb*, or by any name resembling that word. The first mention of cards in Germany calls them *Briefe;* that is to say, *letters*. The first card-makers were named *Brief-maler*.

The Germans composed symbols to mark the suits for themselves, and rejected the Eastern ones, and were probably unconscious that such devices as Hearts, Diamonds, etc., existed on the cards of the neighbouring country; for intercourse in those days was not rapid, and each kingdom was as independent of its fellow as if oceans divided them. M. la Croix says that the Germans "with their love of symbolism discovered a vegetable as well as a military signification in the original game of cards." While making important changes, they retained a little of their warlike character in their symbols and figures, and placed among them some designs inspired by the vegetable world. The devices with them signified the triumphs and the honours of war, and they discarded the weapons of the East, the Swords and the Staves, and disdained the sordid money and the priestly chalice, and adopted sprays of oak and of ivy as if intended for victors' wreaths, and chose tiny bells, or *grelots*, as distinctive marks, as these were among the most important signs of German nobility, and borne by them among the other heraldic marks, and considered most honourable emblems. These symbols gave a more peaceful aspect to the ancient warlike game.

The names of the German suits are *Schellen* (Bells), *Hertzen* (Hearts), *Grün* (Green), and *Eicheln* (Acorns). It is not now known at what period these symbols which have become a distinguishing character of the German cards were adopted, but during part of the fifteenth century other objects were also represented on their cards; and the different marks quarrelled with the others and strove to be generally adopted, but without success, as those named above have been the only ones in use for many generations, although they are now being gradually superseded by the French designs, which among English-speaking nations are known as Hearts, Diamonds, Clubs, and Spades.

Some ancient German packs which have been preserved are not only very remarkable for the beautiful workmanship lavished on their production and as handsome specimens of the engraver's art, but are also curious because they contain five suits instead of the ordinary four. These were divided into *Hares, Parrots, Pinks, Roses*, and *Columbines*, with the usual King, Queen, Knight, and Knave in each suit. These cards were executed in the fifteenth century in the city of Cologne. Other packs of engraved cards made about the latter end of the fifteenth century in Germany had their suits marked by animals, flowers, and birds, and were not coloured, the symbols marking the suits without other aid. The mark of the *Grün*, or Leaf, in the German card resembles in shape the Hearts and Spades of the French. The shape of all these pips is closely analogous; and the Heart provided with a short handle and called a Spade or given a long stem and named a Leaf must originally have had a common origin, all knowledge of which is lost in the mists of the Middle Ages.

The Pique may have received its name of Spade in its English home, not, as some authors fancy, because the word was a corruption of the Spanish *Espadas*, but because it resembled in shape the spade or shovel which was in use in England when cards first made their appearance there. M. la Croix fancies the shape of the *Heart* resembles a shield, and points to this as supporting his claim that the designs on the cards had a military origin. Among the miners in some parts of England *Diamonds* are frequently called *Picks*, owing to their resemblance to the head of that tool. M. la Croix also declares that *les Cœurs* were the symbols placed on the cards by the French adapter, in order to do honour to his friend Jacques Cœur, a merchant of the day whose trade with the East might have been the means of introducing the cards into

France, and fancies that *les Trifles* denoted "the heraldic plant of Agnes Sorel,"—the King's mistress, who had adopted the humble clover-leaf as her badge as a sort of pun upon her own name; the French word *sorel* signifying the plant the leaves of which bear some resemblance to the *Trifle* on the cards.

The *Grelots* on the German cards may have been copied from the "Hawk-bell,"—a favourite mark of nobility, and one which it was considered an honour to be able to display among the symbols on the coat of arms. Bells were also an insignia of rank in India; and some writers have pointed out that the Germans might have copied the devices on their cards from Hindoo packs, as well as from the better known Tarots or Saracen cards. Bells have always been favourite decorations; and their use dates back to the hangings of the Temple, where the fringes which adorned the curtains and the garments of the high-priest were ornamented with bells.

In a beautiful pack of Hindoo cards mentioned by Mr. Singer seven suits were found, consisting of *Suns* represented by golden disks, *Moons* or silver circles, *Crowns*, *Cushions*, *Harps*, *Letters*, and

Swords. These cards closely resemble the Tarots, and may have originated in a common source. In some of the Hindoo packs the suits are distinguished by a colour as well as by the form of the symbol.

Although parts of packs which from the devices they bear may have been imported from Germany or Spain, and which seem to have been well used, are preserved in the British Museum, having been found in England, only cards of French origin have been universally used there, and they have held undisputed sway from the middle of the fifteenth century, when the distinctive colours of red and black, and the emblems of Hearts, Diamonds, Spades, and Clubs were generally adopted, and have remained nearly unchanged from that time to the present. There was no attempt to shade the pips or the figures and faces of the court cards at any time in England, and the outlines were simply coloured and laid on in solid blocks. The French have changed their figures, and shaded their faces, and made their pips slightly more symmetrical in shape; but they are very nearly the same as when originally designed by the clever-fingered French courtier.

CARDS OF DIFFERENT COUNTRIES.

CARDS OF DIFFERENT COUNTRIES.

CHINA.

AS has been already mentioned, the invention of Playing-cards has been claimed at many places; each writer setting forth the pretensions of his own country to this honour to the best of his ability, and each one with seemingly good authority for his statements.

It is certain that the Chinese point in triumph to the longest pedigree for their game, and they quote extensively from their own authors as proof of this fact; and until some European well versed in their language can dispute this claim, it may be as well to allow it.

Mr. Chatto says that cards appear to have been known from an early period in China. There is a Chinese dictionary, entitled "Ching-tsze-tung," compiled by Eul-Kowng, and first published A.D. 1678; which says that the cards now known in China as *Teen-tsze-pae*, or "dotted cards," were invented in the reign of Leun-ho, 1120, and that they began to be common in the reign of Kaow-tsung, who ascended the throne in 1131. According to tradition, they were devised for the amusement of Leun-ho's wives.

The general name for cards in China is *Che-pae*, or "paper-tickets." At first they were called *Ya-pae*, or "bone-tickets," from the material of which they were made. Several varieties of cards seem to be in use in China. One pack that is described by Mr. Chatto is said to be composed of thirty-two cards covered with small circular dots of red and black, with court cards of one man and one woman. The cards most commonly used are called *Tseen-wan-che-pae* (a thousand times ten thousand cards). There are thirty in a pack, divided into three suits of nine cards each, and three single cards, which are superior to all others. The name of one of the suits is *Kew-ko-wan;* that is, "The nine ten thousands" (or "myriads of Kwan," which are strings of beads, shells, or money). The name of the other suit is *Kew-ko-ping* (nine units of cakes); and that of the third, *Kew-ko-so* (nine units of chains). The names of the three single cards are *Tseen-wan* (a thousand times ten thousand),

Heenghwa (the red flower), and *Pi-hwa* (the white flower). One of their games of cards bears the same name as the Chinese game of Chess, *Kew-ma-paon;* and it contains pictures of chariots, horses, and guns.

The Chinese name for a card considered singly or as one of the parts of a pack is *Shen,* or " Fan," — a most evident reference to the manner of holding cards spread open like a fan, which is common to all nations.

The shape and size of the Chinese card are peculiar. They are printed in black on a thin cardboard. The backs are sometimes bright crimson and sometimes black or yellow, and they are the shape and size of a finger. Some of them are little more than half an inch broad by three inches long, and others are an inch wide by three and a half long. The pips and court cards are always printed in black on a white background, and on the face of some of them are stamped Chinese characters printed in red. In some packs the cards have animals, such as horses and deer, represented upon them; while in others characters which may mean the names only of the animals are written above the pips. The cards are rounded at the top and bottom, and at the upper end a small portion is left blank, as if to hold them conveniently and allow of their being spread or "fanned" out, showing the whole of the pictured surface, the blank space being held under the thumb and fingers. Strangely enough, this blank space being at the top instead of at the bottom of the card, it would seem that they should be held by the top and spread out in exactly the reverse way customary among Europeans. The tiny cards are so narrow and so small that they might well be held concealed by the palm of the hand, which could effectually cover them and prevent the shape of the pips being seen through the thin cardboard or the number of the cards being counted by the opponent.

The Chinese have another name for their cards, and this is *Wat-pi;* but it seems to be the name given to different games, as they also call queer-looking tablets on which round dots are placed in regular order and which resemble our dominos, by the same name.

Mr. Singer gives an account of some Chinese cards an inch and a half long and a little more than two inches broad. Each suit consists of nine cards with black backs. They are printed with Chinese characters, and not with emblems like those in other packs.

Some authors state that cards are played by the lower orders only, and that people of distinction play at Chess; and that among the Chinese it is considered undignified to play cards, and many of them pretend they have no idea of their use or the meaning or value of the characters on them.

It is also asserted that a game analogous to the old one of Tarots has been found in China, which contains seventy-seven tablets.

There is a tradition that a Venetian carried cards from China to his native city, which was the first place in Europe where they were known. This traveller was probably Niccolo Polo, who with his brother Matteo returned from China about 1269; or it may have been the celebrated Marco Polo, son of the above Niccolo, who accompanied his father and uncle on their second voyage to that great empire.

EGYPT.

AN attempt has been made to prove that a kind of card was in use among the Egyptians in the seventh century before our present era; but this has been hotly disputed if not disproved. That there were games which were known to the early Egyptians has been shown by the inscriptions on their monuments, and the representations of figures playing jack-stones or knuckle-bones and dice. Some kind of game resembling Chess may also have been played, but upon this subject authorities do not agree.

INDIA.

IF India was not the birthplace of Cards, as it probably was of Chess, it is certain that they were known in that country at a very early date; and beautiful specimens of ancient as well as modern packs are prized in many European collections.

A pack of Hindoo cards is fully described in Mr. Singer's book, and many of them are handsomely reproduced. They are painted on ivory, the backs are gilded, and they number the same as the Tarot cards. This pack contains seven suits, which are *Suns*, *Moons*, *Crowns*, *Cushions*, *Harps*, *Letters*, and *Swords*. Of each of these suits there are ten numeral and two court cards, which appear to represent a Sovereign

Cards of Different Countries.   71

and a General. Besides these there are twelve cards apparently of no suit, on which are groups of figures, some male and some female.

Mr. Chatto describes several packs of Hindostanee cards, among others some owned by the Royal Asiatic Society and preserved in their Museum. One of these packs consists of ten and others of eight suits. "In each suit, when complete, the number of cards is twelve; that is, two coat cards, or honours, and ten others whose numerical value is expressed by the number of marks upon them. The cards of all the packs are circular; the diameter of the largest is two and three quarter inches, and of the smallest about two and an eighth inches." The material of which they are formed is supposed to be canvas, and indeed it is expressly stated in a memorandum that accompanies them that such is the case, but they appear to be made of thin veneers of wood. One of these packs formerly belonged to Capt. D. Cromline Smith, to whom they were presented about 1815 by a high-caste Brahmin, who considered them a great curiosity, and supposed that they were a thousand years old. These cards resemble a pack now owned by Mr. de Forest that he bought in Cashmere within a few years, and that have been reproduced for this work. The Brahmin's pack, says Mr. Chatto, "consists of eight suits, each suit containing two honours and ten common cards, — in all ninety-six cards. In all the suits the King is mounted on an elephant, and in six the Vizir, or second honour, is on horseback; but in the blue suit, the emblem or mark of which is a red spot with a yellow centre, he rides a tiger; and in the white suit, the mark of which appears like a grotesque or fiendish head, he is mounted on a bull. The backs of all the cards are green. The following are the colours of the *ground* on which the figures are painted in the several suits, together with the different marks by which the suits and the respective value of the common cards were also distinguished : —

COLOURS.	MARKS.
1. FAWN.	Something like a pineapple in a shallow cup.
2. BLACK.	A red spot with a white centre.
3. BROWN.	A "tulwar," or sword.
4. WHITE.	A grotesque kind of head.
5. GREEN.	Something like a parasol without a handle, and with two broken ribs sticking through the top.
6. BLUE.	A red spot with a yellow centre.
7. RED.	A parallelogram with dots on it as if to represent writing.
8. YELLOW.	An oval."

Plate 5.

Mr. Chatto mentions other packs with red backs, one of them containing ten suits, and all seemingly distinguished more by the coloured background than the emblem of the suit, which is sometimes entirely omitted, particularly in the court cards. The games to be played are complicated and difficult to understand, although one of them is said to resemble l'Ombre, the favourite game in Spain. The tradition regarding the origin of Hindostanee cards, as given by Mr. Chatto, is "that they were invented by a favourite Sultana or Queen to wean her husband from a bad habit he had acquired of pulling or eradicating his beard." The game of cards is not mentioned in the Arabian Nights, remarks Mr. Chatto, "and from this silence it may be concluded that at the time when those tales were compiled card-playing was not a popular pastime in Arabia. The compilation of these tales, it is believed, is not earlier than about the end of the fifteenth century, although some of them are of a much higher antiquity."

CASHMERE.

THE cards from Cashmere, which belong to Mr. de Forest and are reproduced for this work, differ but slightly from those described by Mr. Chatto. The Cashmere cards are circular in shape, as well as the Hindostanee, and are of about the same size, being two inches in diameter. The emblems on the Cashmere cards differ considerably from those described by Mr. Chatto, and only the court or figure cards bear a general resemblance to those that formerly belonged to Capt. D. Cromline Smith.

The Cashmere cards seem to be made of thin slices of wood, overlaid with a composition of some sort, and so thickly covered with paint and varnish that the original material is entirely concealed. This pack contains thirty-six cards of three suits; namely, ten pip and two court cards in each suit. A large purple flower on a red ground, placed within circles of yellow, ornaments the backs, which are probably intended to be precisely the same; but to an experienced gamester there would be no difficulty in distinguishing one card from another, even with the face of it concealed, as the design, though uniform, differs slightly on each card.

The three suits are not only marked by the emblems of pips, but, like the Hindostanee cards, the backgrounds are vividly painted in some uniform colour upon which the design is displayed, and this colour marks the suits distinctly even when the emblem is omitted, which in some cases is done either by design or accident. The white suit is headed by a King mounted on an elephant, and a Vizir on a bull. There are no emblems on these two cards by which to distinguish the suit. The ten pip cards show tiny figures of men clothed in loosely fitting red garments and wearing red turbans on their heads. These figures are represented kneeling, with their hands clasped in the attitude of prayer. They are dotted over the surface of the cards and grouped as the corresponding pips are in the other suits, and generally face each other, except in number eight, in which all the figures look the same way and to the left side. Another suit is distinguished by a dark-blue ground, on which small yellow disks, surrounded by circles of red, are painted. This suit may correspond with a "moon" suit mentioned by Mr. Chatto among the

Hindostanee cards, and it is also noticeable as it closely resembles the "money" used as an emblem on Italian and Spanish cards. The court cards of this suit show a man mounted on a tiger and bearing the distinctive emblem uplifted in his right hand. The position of this man is closely copied on the Spanish cards, although in them he is represented on horseback. The second honour shows two tigers seated on a cross-legged bench gazing over their shoulders at two attendants, who wave what appear to be staves or fans. Between these tigers is a large "moon-face," which seems to mark the suit. If this be the case, it would point to the origin of the money emblem. The pips on the rest of the suit are carelessly executed circles, and the features, which would show it to be intended for the moon, are omitted. The outline of this mark may have been followed on the cards that were first introduced into Europe, and may readily have become changed during the lapse of years. The "moon" mark on the Hindostanee cards has gradually extended both East and West, one that closely resembles it being found on the Chinese cards, and partly followed on the wooden cubes of the Alaska Indians.

Plate 6.

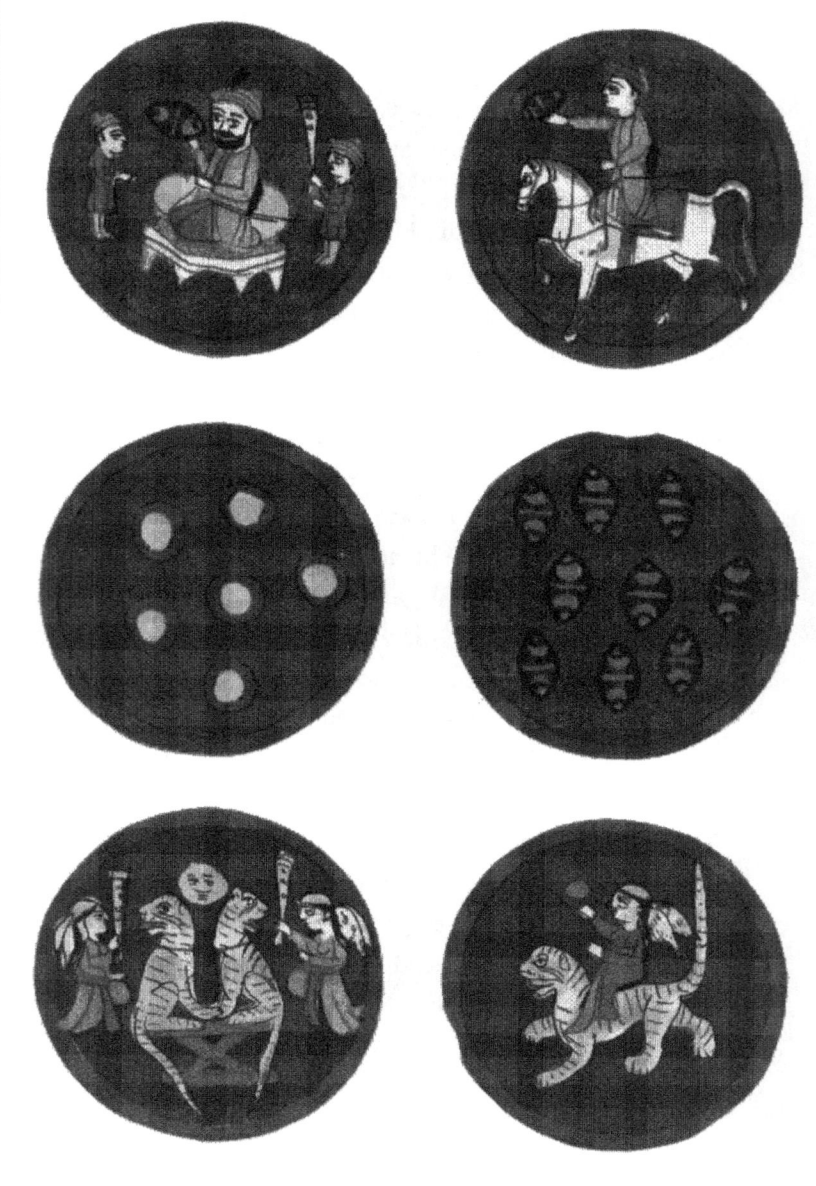

The green suit bears emblems which recall the *carreaux* of the French cards, and are even more like one of the marks used by the Apache tribe of North American Indians by which to distinguish one of their suits. The diamond-shaped pip on the Cashmere cards is painted red and ornamented with stripes and dots of pink. The court cards show a Vizir on a white horse, bearing the pip in his right hand, and a Sultan attended by two slaves, who also carries the emblem of the suit.

These cards show little marks of use, and their surface is slightly sticky, so that they could not be conveniently either shuffled or dealt. It is probable that the pack is not complete, and that there should be more than the three suits that now compose it.

PERSIA.

Six tablets brought from Persia by a recent traveller form an interesting addition to the cards used by different nations. These tiny cards appear to be the three honours of two different packs. They are made of layers of pasteboard, some of them as thick as two ordinary playing-cards. The others are nearly double that thickness; and although they are all of the same size (namely, an inch and an eighth wide by two inches long), there are many marks on them to show that they never all belonged to the same pack. Although made of pasteboard, they are covered so thickly with paint and varnish that they might easily be supposed to have been cut out of wood. The backs of these cards are all alike, and are painted black. They are remarkable for the female figure that they bear as a court card, as in this respect they are not only unlike all other Eastern cards, but in it differ from those of every Western nation, with the exception of the French and those other countries where the French cards have been adopted. This female figure is by some called a Courtesan, but it could as well be named a Queen. She is seated on a chair of state, that is ornamented with a design which closely resembles one of the emblems used on a Hindostanee pack of cards, and which is called a crown by Mr. Chatto. This may, however, be a purely accidental resemblance. A young child is placed in the lap of this Queen, but she bears no particularly distinctive emblems either on her dress or on any part of the card which might serve to mark the suit. The background of one of these Queens is yellow, and that of the other one is red, and there are two Queens in this pack of six cards. There are two cards which appear to belong to the " Yellow Queen." One of them shows a Hunter on a golden background drawing his knife across the throat of some animal; and the other card bears a Cavalier mounted on a white horse, on the back of which is perched a tiger. This card has a black background. A sun placed at the top may be intended for the distinguishing emblem. These three cards undoubtedly belong to the same pack, and are considerably thicker than the others, which are much more highly ornamented and better finished than those already described. The Queen is handsomely dressed; her hair is covered, and she wears large ear-rings, from which depend a necklace. The child is dressed in a loosely fitting garment, and its head is covered with a jewelled cap. The background of this card is a beautiful red, and the corners are ornamented with fine arabesques of flowers and fruit. The King which belongs to this set is accompanied by a female figure, and they are placed on a yellow background, but they bear no emblem by which they might be distinguished. The third card has a very richly ornamented golden background, and shows two figures, one of them carrying what appears to be a drum. All these cards have beautifully ornamented corners, and are painted like a miniature.

ITALY.

THE first European document known that mentions cards is the manuscript already referred to, written by Nicolas de Covellezzo, about the end of the thirteenth century, is preserved among the archives of Viterbo, and contains the earliest written account yet discovered of cards, not only among the Italians but also in Europe, if we except the much disputed passage in the Wardrobe Rolls of Edward the First, King of England, which will hereafter be mentioned. This document refers to cards by the name of *Carte*, as well as by that of *Naïbi*.

Mr. Singer says that "the first game played in

Plate 7.

Italy was without question Trappola. This had been introduced from Arabia, and is mentioned by many early Italian authors, one of whom writing in 1393 calls cards *Naïbi*, and speaks contemptuously of them as a childish game. Another writer, Tenanza, declares that in 1441 the Venetian Maître-cartiers, who formed a large guild, remonstrated with the Senate of that city on the injury done to their trade by the importation of large quantities of playing-cards with printed as well as painted figures within their gates, which had been manufactured elsewhere; and this remonstrance shows that the card-makers of the day were already numerous, and seems to point to the fact that the use of cards was well established, and that considerable numbers were called for and manufactured."

Lorenzo de' Medici mentions the games of La Bassetta and Il Frusso in some of his "Canzoni," printed before 1492; and there are Italian writers who point to him as the inventor of some games of cards.

In Italy the suits were called *Coppe* (Cups), *Spadi* (Swords), *Denari* (Money), *Bastoni* (Maces). These continued to be the commonly used marks on the

Italian cards from the sixteenth century to a much later period; and the same suits and pips have been used in Spain from the time of their first history to the present day. An Italian writer claims that a native of Bologna invented Tarots or Tarocchino before the year 1419, and says that "there is preserved in the Fibbia family, which was one of the most illustrious and ancient of that city, a portrait of Francis Fibbia, Prince of Pisa, who sought refuge at Bologna about the commencement of the fifteenth century, in which he is represented holding in his right hand a parcel of cards, while others appear lying at his feet. Among the latter are seen the Queen of *Batons* and the Queen of *Denari;* the one bearing the arms of the Bentivoglio family, and the other the arms of the Fibbia. An inscription at the bottom of the picture states that Francis Fibbia, who died in 1419, had obtained as the inventor of Tarocchino, from the *Reformers* of the city, the privilege of placing his own arms on the Queen of *Batons*, and that of his wife, who was one of the Bentivoglio family, on the Queen of *Denari*. Writers disagree as to whether Fibbia invented the emblems of the cards or joined two packs of cards which already had their appropriate emblems into one, or whether he invented a new game to be played with the already well known Tarocchino cards.

Notice should be taken of the fact that printed as well as painted cards are mentioned in the petition of the card-makers of Venice, as it was from this date that each village in Italy manufactured its own cards. After the invention of wood-engraving, Germany and Holland exported cards in large quantities, and this may have called for the protective decree. There was also a difference, which was mentioned in the documents of the period, between the primitive *Naïbi* and cards proper. As these documents do not define the difference between the packs, we can form no idea of what it was.

GERMANY.

IN a German book printed at Augsburg in 1472, called "Gülden Spiel," or "The Golden Game," written by a Dominican friar of the name of Ingold, it is stated that cards had been known in Germany since 1300. As this is by no means contemporaneous testimony, it is probable that the German vanity which claims the honor of inventing the art of printing wishes, with no more reason on its side, to appropriate to itself the invention of playing-cards, which in plain words is laying claim to the invention of wood-engraving, as many of the early German packs are engraved and not stencilled or painted. This rather suspicious assertion may therefore well be ignored, and we may only credit the one made by the Italian author of Viterbo, which is apparently more authentic. Unfortunately, the latter gives no details about the kind of cards which he mentions. He only states that cards made their appearance in 1379 in Europe, and came from Arabia under their original name.

In the "Livre d'Or" of Ulm, which is a manuscript preserved in that city, there is an ordinance, dated 1397, forbidding all card-playing.

These are the only authentic witnesses that can be brought forward by which the approximate time of the introduction of playing-cards into Europe may be fixed.

A German author by the name of Heniken claims for his country the birthplace of cards, and brings forward many ingenious but hardly satisfac-

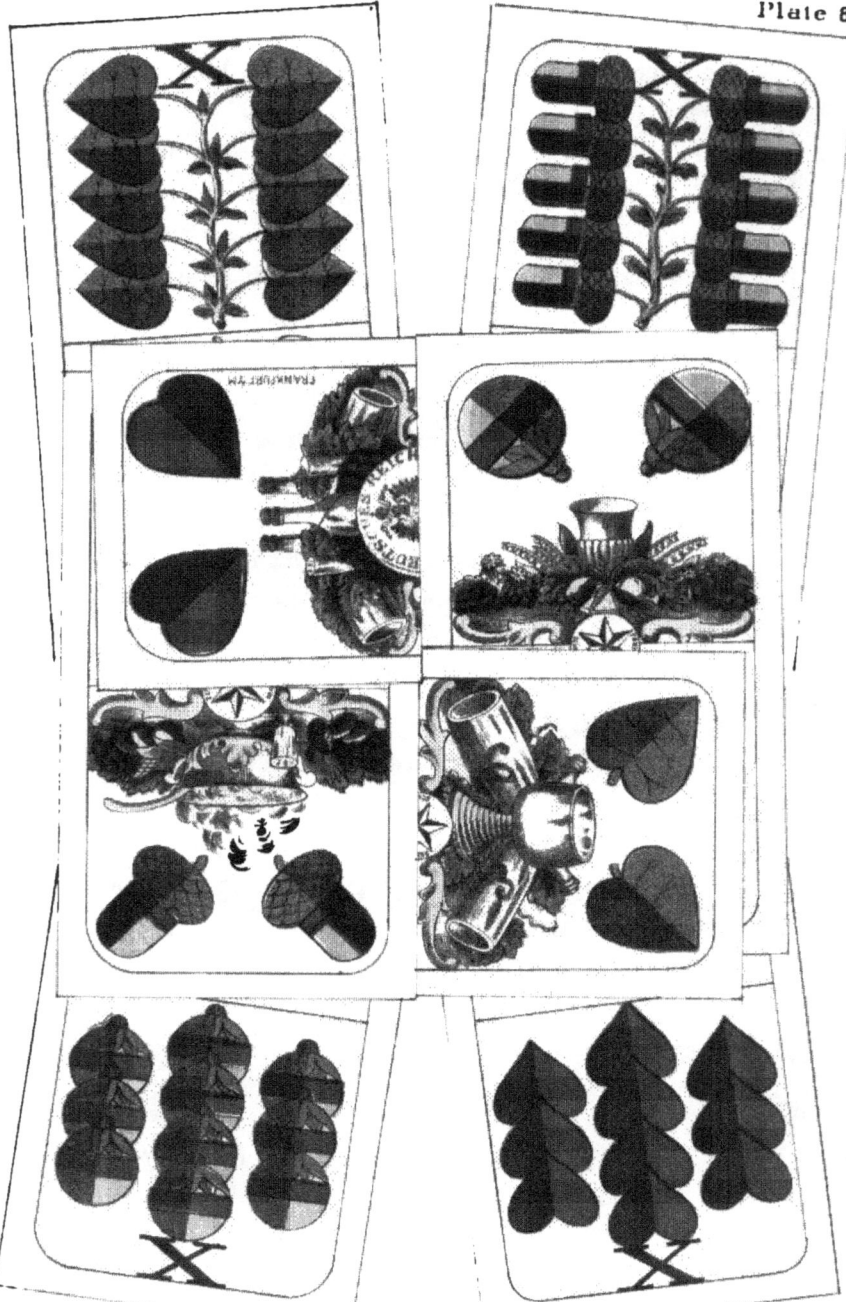

Plate 8.

tory deductions in support of his pretensions. He says that *Briefe*, which is the name that cards bear in his country, means "letters," and that the common people do not say, "Give me a pack of cards," but "Give me a *Spiel-briefe*" (a pack of letters), and they do not say, "I want a *card*," but "I want a *Brief*" (letter). "We should at least have preserved the name *carte*," he says, "if they had come to us from France; for the common people always preserve the names of all games that come to them from other countries."

Unfortunately for this argument, it has been discovered that cards were called *Karten* in Germany before they were called *Briefe*. It may be claimed that cards were carried into Germany by the Crusaders, who had learned their use during the wars with the Saracens. They might also have made an ingenious use of the cards during their long absences in the East, and diverted them from their original purposes, writing letters to mothers, wives, or sweethearts on them, or chosen them to send to the young folk at home to serve for their amusement, as the pictures of the Kings, Knights, etc., rude though they probably were, would have undoubtedly proved both novel and entertaining; and from this fact the name of *Briefe* may have been given to the *Naïbi* of the Orient. The Eastern origin of the cards is plainly pointed to, as there are no Queens in ancient packs of German cards.

In many parts of Germany the court and pip cards which are usually used resemble most closely those which are represented in the packs of the early part of the fifteenth century. The cards which are at the present time (1890) manufactured at Frankfort in Germany are copies of the French packs of the fifteenth century, with the modifications which have crept in during the lapse of over three hundred years; and they display the modern Hearts, Diamonds, Clubs, and Spades, and these cards are generally used in the German Empire. But the same factory turns out cards which are suited to the more conservative portions of the country, where the ancient *Schellen* (Bells), *Hertzen* (Hearts), *Grün* (Green), and *Eicheln* (Acorns) are still preferred.

In the modern German cards each Ace bears the attributes of the wine-cellar or the *biergarten*. In the ancient cards the Ace was always draped with a flag. The modern *Hearts* are surrounded with champagne bottles. *Acorns* carry a loving-cup; *Bells*, a steaming punch-bowl; and *Leaves*, beer-glasses and goblets. There are no Queens in this pack, their place being taken by Knights on horseback dressed in beautiful uniforms; and beside their heads is the word *Ober*, signifying the position they hold over the Knaves, which are represented as working-men. There are only five pip cards in this pack, numbered from five to ten; and the emblems are arranged in a symmetrical and fanciful way, quite unlike the cards which were adapted by the French from the original Tarots and adopted by all English-speaking nations. The backs of these cards bear a plaid or checkered pattern, recalling to mind those of the original Tarots.

To a German is due the adaptation of cards to the instruction of children; and this idea, which was promulgated soon after the first introduction of these packs into Germany, has been developed steadily through successive years, until now it is possible to study history, geography, and other sciences by these means, and babies still in the nursery learn to spell and to read after a fashion by playing the various games which are strewn before their unappreciative eyes. The name of this ingenious inventor was Thomas Murer, a Franciscan friar, who in 1507 arranged a game in which various branches of education were taught. Each card was covered with so many symbols that M. la Croix declares that "their description alone resembles the most gloomy rebus;" but the German universities, undaunted by difficulties, enjoyed the study of logic and other sciences under the guise of amusement, and Murer's game was imitated and continues to be so to the present time.

SPAIN.

THE Spaniards base their claim of having been the first to use, if they were not the inventors of, playing-cards to the fact that *Naïbi*, the name by which cards were known among the Italians about the year 1393, is very nearly similar to the name by which they are known in Spain to-day. As it was about that time that Italy was invaded by the Spaniards, they declare that they, as the conquerors, imposed cards upon that country and taught their use, under the name they bore in their own homes.

The Spanish word *Naïpes*, as we have already mentioned, seems to be derived from one which means "flat" or "even;" but an ancient Spanish dictionary states that it comes from the initial letters of the name of the Spanish inventor of cards, N. P., Nicolas Pepin. This etymology seems fanciful and as unsatisfactory as the claim to the invention of the cards; but the Spaniards can point to a statute made by John the First, King of Castile, in 1387, which prohibits "games of dice, of Naypes, and of Chess;" and this proves beyond dispute that at that date they were at least well known in that place.

A Flemish traveller named Eckeloo, who lived about 1540, describes the Spaniards of his time as "most passionately fond of gambling," and says that he "travelled many leagues in Spain without being able to procure the necessaries of life, not even bread or wine, but that in every miserable village cards were to be bought." Travellers of the present day describe the tradespeople, fishermen, and beggars of every wretched town playing even at the street-corners, and using blocks of stone or the steps of the churches on which to throw their cards.

It was the Spaniards without doubt who carried cards into Mexico, when they conquered that country in 1519; and history mentions that Montezuma took great pleasure in watching the Spanish soldiers at their games.

Mr. Singer says that the Spanish pack consists, like the German, of only forty-eight cards, as they contain no *tens*. Their four suits are named *Espadas* (Spades), *Copas* (Cups), *Oros* (Money), and *Bastos* (Maces). *Oros* means literally "golden money;" and this suit is also called *Dineros*, — that is, "money in general." Like the Italian and German packs, they have no Queen, her place being taken by the usual Knight, or Mounted horseman. The court cards are called *Il Rey* (King), *Caballo* (Knight), and *Sota* (Knave). There are some packs in which a Queen is permitted, the suits then having four court cards instead of three.

FRANCE.

AMONG the archives preserved in the Chambre des Comptes in Paris there was at one time an account, dated 1392, which said, "Paid to Jacquemin Gringonneur, Painter, for three packs of cards

Plate 9.

of gold and different colours, ornamented with different devices for the King [Charles the Sixth], for his amusement, 50 sols parisis."

The game, which was invented merely as an amusement for the deranged King, spread with such rapidity among the people that the Prevôt de Paris, in an ordinance dated Jan. 22, 1397, was obliged to "forbid working people from playing tennis, ball, *cards*, or ninepins, excepting only on holidays." Especial notice should be taken of the fact that in a celebrated and oft-quoted ordinance made only twenty-eight years previously by Charles the Fifth, in which all games of hazard were enumerated, no allusion whatever was made to *cards*, while in the fifteenth century they are always carefully mentioned when games of chance are enumerated. By this we can place approximately the date of their invention or introduction into France.

Although packs of Tarots have survived since the fifteenth century, and one in particular will be described, there are no existing specimens of the original Tarots (Tarocchi, Tarocchini); but there is a pack which was engraved by a burin (or graving-tool), that probably was executed about the year

1460, which is known to be an exact copy of the first Tarots.

Rafael Maffie, who lived at the end of the fifteenth century, left in his "Commentaries" a description of Tarots, which were then, said he, "a new invention;" but he probably was speaking relatively of the origin of cards. From his description and the documents of others it is clear that the pack of Tarots was composed of four or five suits, each one of the ten cards being numbered in sequence, and displaying as their symbols the Denari, the Bastoni, the Coppe, and the Spade; and these suits were headed by the court cards of King, Knight, and Knave, to which was sometimes added a Queen. Besides these cards, which were *en suite*, there were others which bore fanciful figures, and which were named Atouts. The Tarots have been so fully described in another place that it is not necessary to repeat the description here.

A very slight knowledge of the history of playing-cards reveals the fact that Tarots were known in France long before the invention of the game of Piquet, which is undoubtedly of French origin; and besides this, the cards which are said to have belonged to Charles the Sixth are Tarots, and must be classed as such. They are preserved in the Cabinet des Estampes de la Bibliothèque Nationale de Paris, and they may be looked upon with respect as being the oldest in any collection, public or private. Although nearly five hundred years of age, they are well preserved.

Besides the Tarot pack, which is supposed to have been one of the three packs that were painted by Gringonneur, there are preserved in the same museum parts of another old pack which show distinctly that they are of a later date. These cards are essentially French, and are not to be classed among the Tarots. There are a King, Queen, and Knave in each suit. Their Saracenic origin may still be traced, as they bear the crescent of the Mussulman instead of the carreau (diamond) of the Frenchman; and the Club is shaped after the Arabic or Moorish fashion, which had four equal branches, like a four-leaved clover, instead of the three leaves that were afterward adopted as the distinctive symbol of the suit.

Another noticeable peculiarity is that the King of Hearts is represented as a monkey covered with hair or skins, and he leans on a knobby staff.

The Queen of his suit is dressed in skins like her consort, and in one hand she carries a torch. It would seem natural that the Knave of Hearts should be dressed to correspond with the royal personages belonging to his suit; but instead it is the Knave of Clubs who is represented as covered with hair or dressed in skins, and he carries a knotty stick over one shoulder. A part of another card has been found among those that the book-binder's knife has separated from the proper body (for these cards, like so many of their kind, once formed part of the binding of a book); and this one shows the legs only of a fourth hairy person. The upper part has unfortunately never been found.

With the exception of these savages, all the other figures of the pack are dressed after the fashion of the court of Charles the Seventh of France. The costume of the Queen of Diamonds resembles that of Marie d'Anjou, his consort. The figures of the Kings, with the exception of the hairy one, are dressed precisely like the pictures of Charles the Seventh or the lords of his court. They wear a velvet hat surmounted by a crown formed of fleurs-de-lis, with a coat opened in front and bordered with ermine. The doublet is tight-fitting, and the boots extremely high. The dresses of the Knaves are copies of those worn by the pages and the sergent-d'armes of the period. One of them wears a plumed cap and a long coat with flowing sleeves. The other Knave is in court dress, and is the complete opposite of his fellow, as he wears a closely fitting doublet. The latter carries a banner on which is displayed the name of the manufacturer, F. Clerc. It seems therefore safe to conclude that these cards are of French origin. And now occurs an interesting question, which is, how it is possible to explain the presence of the savage King, Queen, and Knave among the other court cards, which are all dressed in the height of the fashion of the period of Charles the Seventh; but if the history of the preceding reign is referred to, the probable solution of this enigma will be found.

On the 29th of February, 1392, a grand fête was held in the palace of Queen Blanche, given in honour of the marriage of the Chevalier Vermandois to one of her Majesty's maids of honour. The King, Charles the Sixth, who had been for some time in a melancholy state of mind which sometimes amounted to madness, was for the time being enjoying a lucid interval, and was induced to enter into a frolic which was proposed by one of his favourite courtiers by the name of Hugonin de Janzay. It was arranged that in this masquerade the King and five of his lords should take part. "It was," says Juvenal des Ursins, "a *momerie* of savage men, heavily chained and dressed in *justes au corps* made of linen which had been greased and covered with hairs, and which was made to fit close to the body." Froissart, who was an eyewitness of this fête, says that "the six actors in the dance rushed into the ball-room howling and shaking their clattering chains." As no one was able to recognize the hairy monsters, so well were they disguised, the Duc d'Orleans, the King's brother, seized a lighted torch from the hands of an attendant, and pressed it so closely against one of these strange people that the light set fire to the linen coat, which blazed up immediately. By great good fortune the King had become separated from his companions, all of whom with only one exception were roasted alive. This lucky chevalier rushed from the room, and flung himself head first into a vat full of water and thus saved his life. Charles indeed escaped; but the horrors of the situation, combined with the terror, fatigue, and grief to which it gave rise, so impressed his already enfeebled mind that he became hopelessly insane.

The Ballet des Ardents left such a vivid impression on the public mind that sixty years later a German engraver made it the subject of a print, so that it is not hazarding an inadmissible guess to fancy that a card-maker of the day should seize upon it for a subject, particularly as the cards of the period were sometimes decorated like the horrible Dance of Death, as if they were intended to awaken in the mind of the roystering player some thoughts which might lead him to dwell on more serious subjects, and by means of the cards to reach persons who might otherwise never be drawn to think of them.

There is another and very important fact which must not be overlooked when we are endeavoring to trace a resemblance between the savages depicted on the cards and the personages of the day. The Queen of Hearts is represented as a wild woman holding a torch; and it may be remembered that Isabella of Bavaria, the wife of Charles the Sixth, had agreed to this fatal masquerade, and had encouraged it by her presence, and that this frolic came very near relieving her of her insane consort. Her accomplice in this scheme was the Duc d'Orleans, her brother-in-law, who may have intentionally set fire to the inflammable clothes of these savages, among whom was the King. The gossip of the day certainly accused these two persons with having designed the masquerade with the hope of ridding themselves of the King, whose life interfered greatly with their infamous projects.

Having described what is perhaps the oldest pack of cards which have been preserved, attention must be drawn to another — or rather a fragment of a pack — which is very little, if any, younger than the set already studied. These cards can be traced back to the same period as the first, and are identified by the costumes of the court. They bear great similarities to the modern cards, and are supposed to have been the Adams and Eves of the card world. These are absolutely the first specimens of the French suit cards; the marks of the pips, Clubs, Hearts, Spades, and Diamonds are here displayed for the first time; and if not the pack rearranged by the French courtier, they must have been manufactured at the same time. In these the Kings, Queens, and Knaves bear attributes as well as symbols. The first-named carry spears, and the Queens flowers, and everything in the pictures reflects the fashions of the period; and in them can be discovered no violation of the laws of heraldry or the customs of chivalry.

Tradition points to this pack as that first used in Piquet. It dethroned the Italian Tarots and the cards of Charles the Sixth, and was the ancestor of the present cards. It is believed that they were the invention of Étienne Vignoles, or La Hire, one of the bravest and most active warriors of the day. M. la Croix declares that this tradition should receive respectful attention, because even a cursory examination of the game of Piquet shows that it could only have been the work of an accomplished knight, or have at least originated in a mind intimately acquainted with chivalrous manners and customs. But this charming French author points to another courtier, a contemporary and friend of Vignoles, who might have made the ingenious discovery or invention which resulted in the overthrow of the ancient Tarots; and this was Étienne Chevalier, secretary and treasurer to the King, and famous for his talent for designing, who was one of the cleverest draughtsmen of his day, and who was perfectly capable of rearranging the pack, introducing a Queen in place of the Vizir or Knight, and adopting symbolic colours and distinguishing devices to mark the suits.

The original cards may perhaps have been imported into France and introduced at court by one Jacques Cœur, whose commercial relations with the East were so extensive that he was even accused of supplying the Saracens with arms. In India the cards represented the game of the Vizir and of War, but under the hands of the royal secretary it became the game of the Knight and of Chivalry. He placed on the cards the unicorn which is often found in old packs; nor did he forget to do honour to Jacques Cœur in substituting *les cœurs* for *les coupes*. He changed the *deniers* (money) to diamonds (or arrow-heads), and spears to spades. He may have adapted his designs from those on the German cards, as they bear hearts like the French packs; and a few strokes of the pencil would convert the acorn of the former into the club of the latter. The affinity between the cards of the two countries is quite apparent, but to whom we owe the invention is undecided.

It was in December, 1581, or in the reign of Henry the Third, that the first laws which fix the standing of the *fesseurs de cartes* are found. These statutes, which were confirmed by letters-patent in 1584 and 1613, remained in force until the Revolution. When the privileges of the Corporation were confirmed in 1613, a rule was made that the master card-makers should henceforth and forever put their names, surnames, seals, and devices on the *Valet de Trifle* (Knave of Clubs) in each pack of cards, — a rule which only followed and confirmed an ancient custom, and one which is adopted to the present day.

The modern French cards differ slightly from those used in England and America, as they are smaller, and the edges are rounded and generally gilded. The cards, instead of being perfectly flat, are slightly curved; and this is in order to facilitate shuffling, which is not done in France in the way usually adopted among English-speaking nations, where the pack is divided and laid on a flat surface, and the edges of the cards are lifted and allowed to pass quickly one over the other, in this way distributing or shuffling them very rapidly. The French cards are divided, but held up, and the sides of the two parts pressed together, which shuffles them effectually, but which it is impossible to do if the cards are not curved.

ENGLAND.

SOME of the most interesting collections of old playing-cards can be seen in the Bodleian Library at Oxford, the South Kensington Museum, and the British Museum in London. The latter collection has a historian of its own; and the variety, number, and beauty of the packs in this place are minutely recorded, and form an interesting study by themselves. By their aid it is possible to note the various changes and modifications which have crept in among the costumes of the court, and the pips of the suit cards. The early packs seem to have been imported from Spain, as they bear the old symbols of *coin*, *maces*, *swords*, and *cups*. Other

Plate 10.

packs have been found which were stencilled with the *grelots* (bells) commonly found on the early German cards; but finally the French card came into common use, and these were adopted and have been universally accepted in England, and by her introduced into her colonies, so that these marks of Hearts, Diamonds, Clubs, and Spades are found all over the globe.

The English and American card of the present day differs slightly from those in use in France. The latter have discarded obsolete costumes and fanciful devices when designing the figures of the court cards, and the dresses are modernized, the faces are shaded, and the whole figure looks more like a pretty picture than the cherished card dear to the heart of the Englishman, whose Kings are dressed somewhat after the fashion of Henry the Eighth, the Queens like his mother, Elizabeth of York, and the Knaves in the costume adopted by the lower classes in the days of Chaucer.

It is perhaps to the overthrow of the court-card family during the French Revolution that this radical change in their costumes is due. When the monarchs of the suits were beheaded and their places taken by the sages, philosophers, etc., of the day, it was natural that the obsolete costumes should disappear with them, and that when the royalties of card-land returned to their thrones, the card-maker should adopt the costumes then in fashion in which to clothe the royal family. There having been no such disaster in England, the Kings of the cards have peacefully ruled for several hundred years, clad in the garments of their ancestors, which have only become quainter and more peculiar with the lapse of years, so that now they are often merely lines and dots, and are hardly to be recognized as ermine-trimmed garments which were originally covered with correct heraldic devices.

The first introduction of cards into England (for it has never been claimed that they were invented there) is a matter of dispute; but it is probable that they were known in that country soon after the Second Crusade, at the latter end of the thirteenth century. A passage has been found in the Wardrobe Rolls of Edward the First (1278) which is pointed to by some writers who wish to prove that cards were adopted in England before they were known in other countries; and they claim that this is the earliest mention of a game of cards in any authenticated register. In this

Plate II.

account is recorded the following passage: "Waltero Sturton ad opus regis ad ludendum ad *Quatuor Reges* viii. s. vd." But it by no means follows that "Four Kings" meant cards; it might have been any game, and may have been intended for Chess played with four armies, each one headed by a king, — a game which is by no means obsolete, and which has already been described. Edward the First had served in Syria for five years before his accession to the throne of England, and some writers assert that he brought cards home with him; but Chaucer, who died in 1400, never mentions cards, although in enumerating the amusements of the day he says, —

"They dancen and they play at chess and tables."

The year 1465 is the earliest date at which any positive mention is made of cards in England, and this was in a law which forbade their use except at certain specified times and seasons.

It is probable that cards first made their way into the country from Spain, as the oldest packs which have been found in England bear the symbols of *cups, money, maces, swords;* and the word *spade* (the Spanish name for one of their suits) seems to have become attached to the French *pique* after the cards of the latter nation became domiciled in the British Isles.

Mr. Singer, quoting from another author, says that " there is little doubt but that the cards used during the reign of Philip and Mary and probably the more early part of Elizabeth's were Spanish, though they were afterwards changed for the French, being of a more simple figure and more easily imported." The wars between England and France, during which the army of the former nation were in their sister country, may have led to the adoption of the French card; but it is strange that the costumes on the English cards should date from an earlier period than the reign of Mary or Elizabeth.

" Queen Elizabeth as well as her sister Mary," says Mr. Chatto, " was a card-player," and lost her temper over the game, in which she did not resemble Queen Anne of Austria, of whom one of her ladies-in-waiting, Madame de Motteville, says: " She played like a queen, without passion of greed or gain." During Elizabeth's reign, in 1582, the Master of the Revels was commanded "to show on St. Stephen's day at night before her Majesty at Wyndesore a Comodie or Morral devised on a game of the cardes," to be performed by the children of her Majesty's Chapel. In the comedy "Alexander and Campaspe," which was shown by the same children at Windsor before the Queen, was the following pretty little song, quoted by Mr. Chatto: —

> "Cupid and my Campaspe played
> At cards for kisses. Cupid paid.
> He stakes his quiver, bow, and arrows,
> His mother's doves, and team of sparrows;
> Loses them too; then down he throws
> The coral of his lip, the rose
> Growing on 's cheek (but none knows how);
> With these the chrystal on his brow
> And then the dimple of his chin; —
> All these did my Campaspe win.
> At last he set her both his eyes.
> She won, and Cupid blind doth rise.
> Oh, Love, has she done this to thee?
> What shall, alas! become of me?"

"It is probable that Primero was one of the earliest games of cards played in England," says Mr. Singer; "and it continued to be the most fashionable one throughout the reigns of Henry the Eighth, Edward the Sixth, Mary, Elizabeth, and James." Shakspeare makes Falstaff say, —

> "I never prospered since I forswore myself at Primero;"

showing that it was a well known game at that period. "An alteration or improvement of this game became," says the same author, "known as El Hombre (The man), or Ombre, which is the national game of Spain." It was played generally by three persons, at small three-cornered tables; and these little card-tables are frequently found among collections of old furniture.

That Ombre, or its successor, Quadrille, was a fashionable game at no very ancient period, is proved by the inimitable description given in Cranford of the card-parties held in that mildewed little place. It says: "The drawing-rooms contained small tables, on which were displayed a kaleidoscope, conversation cards, puzzle cards (tied together to an interminable length with faded pink satin ribbon). The card-table was an animated scene to watch,—four old ladies' heads, with niddle-noddling caps all nearly meeting over the middle of the table in their eagerness to whisper quick enough and loud enough, 'Basto, madam, you have Spadille, I believe.'"

A game much in favour among the common folks at the latter end of the sixteenth century was, says Singer, "an old one called Trump, which was prob-

Plate 12.

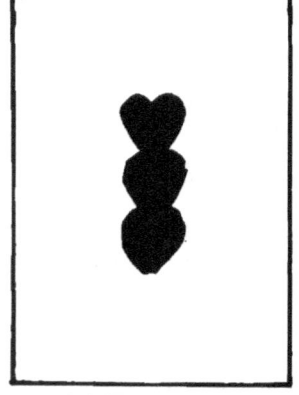

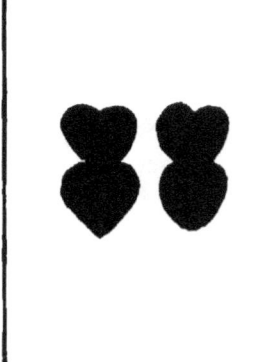

ably the Triumfo of the Spaniards and Italians." In that amusing performance "Gammer Gurton's Needle," first acted in 1561, Dame Chat says to Diccon, —

"We sat at *trump* man by the fire;"

and afterward to her maid she says, —

"There are five *trumps* besides the Queen."

Trump bore some resemblance to Whist or Ruff (another name for that game); and it is noticeable that these two words should still be used in playing Whist, and that both of them signify the same thing. We are told by Mr. Singer that Whist and Honours (alias Slam) were games commonly known in all parts of England, and that "every child of eight years old has competent knowledge in that recreation."

In a book published in 1787, called "The Complete Gamester," by Richard Seymour, Esq., we find the following sentence: "Whist, vulgarly called *Whisk*, is said to be a very ancient game among us, and the foundation of all English games upon the cards." It was probably invented about the period of Charles the Second. Its original name was Whist, or the Silent game. It is believed that "it was not played upon principles until about 1736; before that time it was chiefly confined to servants' halls. The rules laid down by the gentlemen who frequented the Crown Coffee House in Bedford Row were: 'To play from a straight suit; to study your partner's hand as much as your own; never to force your partner unnecessarily, and to attend to the score.'" At one time it was usual to deal four cards together. Horace Walpole, writing in 1767 from Paris, says: "The French have adopted the two dullest things the English have, — Whist and Richardson's novels."

The Whist-players of the last century would be astonished to see the developments a hundred years have made in this game. At the present time the books which have been written on it alone would fill a small book-case, — the one by "Cavendish," who is the acknowledged authority on the game, having reached its seventeenth edition; and it has become so complicated that its rules require profound study, and so fashionable that teachers of its mysteries have sprung up in all directions. Several ladies have adopted the profession of Whist-teachers, and have found it a most profitable one. One person has reduced the system of teaching it to a science, and has also invented an arrangement by which "a singleton" can play a four-handed game of Whist. This is done by placing an ingenious combination of letters and figures on the backs of the ordinary playing-cards, which can be sorted according to these instead of being dealt in the usual way. The cards having been sorted are placed face downward on the table, and then turned up in regular order exactly as if played by four persons. As they have been arranged so as to illustrate certain styles of play or exemplify well known rules, the games they play are not only most amusing, but also instructive. The credit of this novel invention is due to Mr. Frederic Foster, a well known teacher of the noble game of Whist; and his pack is known as the "Self-playing Cards."

The national games of the different countries are said to be: Italy, *Minchiate;* Germany, *Landsknechtspiel,* or Lansquenet; France, *Piquet;* Spain, *El Hombre;* America, *Poker.*

AMERICA.

THE history of Playing-cards would be incomplete without some reference to their introduction into America, and a slight sketch of the games most in favour in that country. History tells us that Columbus carried cards with him in his ship on the voyage of discovery in 1492, and that his sailors employed every spare moment playing with them, until their superstitious fancies persuaded them that this impious practice was the cause of the long voyage and contrary winds which alarmed them so greatly. During the frenzy caused by this panic, they flung overboard their Jonahs (the cards). Their safe arrival at what they believed to be the Promised Land caused them to forget their fears, and they soon regretted the rashness with which they had sacrificed their beloved amusement; so with considerable ingenuity they made for themselves new packs from the leaves of the copas-tree. Tradition states that the sacrificed cards had been made of leather. The introduction of cards into America, their first makers, and the materials

Plate 13.

Sir Jeffery Amherst's Compliments to Mrs. Bush Miller and desires the Favour of her Company to a Ball, at the New Assembly Room, on Saturday the 23d Instant, being the Anniversary of St. George.

Head-Quarters, April 18, 1763.

used, are therefore matters of history, and call for no research or speculation.

A few years after the discovery of America, another history relates that on the conquest of Mexico, and during the captivity of her unfortunate king, Montezuma, he was deeply interested in watching the games of cards played by the conquerors in his presence.

The Spanish marks of suits are now to be found on the cards used in Mexico; but the inhabitants of that country are gradually adopting the French marks used in their sister republic, the United States, and the old cards will soon be as obsolete as their forefathers, the Tarots.

In those parts of the United States that were first settled by religious fanatics it would be useless to search for any record of cards, as they were looked upon with horror by both the Puritans and the Quakers, and together with all games, such as Chess, Draughts, etc., were considered inventions of the Evil One, and their use was sternly forbidden; and it is more than probable that the famous "Mayflower," which seems to have contained enough furniture (judging from the alleged specimens preserved) to have filled an ordinary-sized town, did not contain one card-table or pack of playing-cards. It was natural, however, that some amusement should be craved by the younger members of society, and that games which were considered more harmless than the "Devil's books" (as cards were named by the Puritans) should have been sought for and discovered. Among these were the various kinds of instructive cards which had been invented so many years previously by the Franciscan friar, and which had met with so much favour in parts of Europe. These cards taught various branches of science to the player, and were very numerous; and packs of them by degrees forced their way into different places where the wicked French cards, with their royal dames and kings and their scampish knaves, — whose names alone were synonymous with wrongdoing, gambling, and thieving, — and the innocent-looking but bad little pips, were strictly forbidden.

One quaint pack of Educational Cards, which seems to have been made in America and probably in New York, has been carefully preserved for nearly one hundred years, and is most valuable as giving specimens of the cards used at that

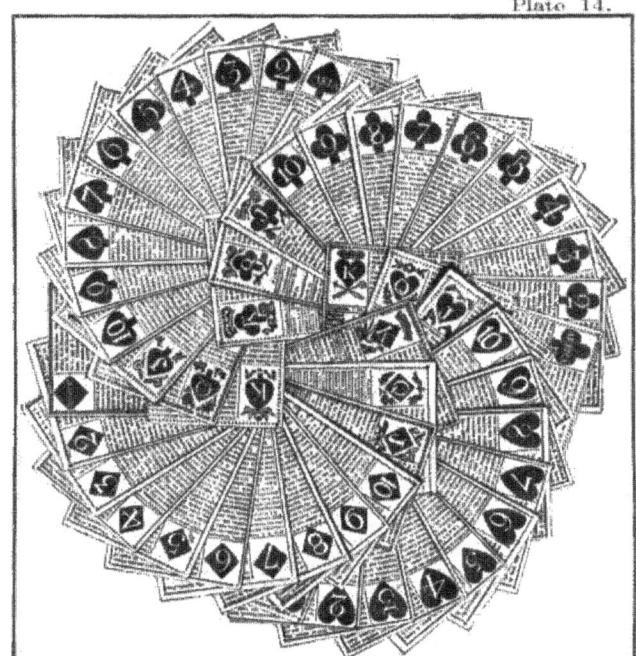

Plate 14.

time. This pack is now owned by Dr. Richard Derby, a descendant of the Lloyd who was granted the manor of Lloyd's Neck, which was one of the original manors (or grants of land) held under the English in the colony of New York; and these cards are preserved in the family mansion on Lloyd's Neck, Long Island. Tied in a pack by a crumpled green ribbon,— which tradition declares was a garter, — on the back of the Knave of Diamonds is written in faded ink this inscription, —

> To Angelina Lloyd, from her affectionate Uncle,
> HENRY LLOYD.
> February 13th, 1795.

The cards (which are wonderfully fresh) are printed on coarse, thick pasteboard, guiltless of enamelled surface or diapered back. The descriptive matter is printed with fine type on each card, which has either a distinguishing pip containing a number on each left-hand upper corner, or in a lozenge is a letter, K, Q, or J, which takes the place of the figure usually placed on the court cards of each suit.

The suits represent the four quarters of the globe. Clubs contain a history of Africa (the name being printed across the surface of the cornered Ace), — its area, inhabitants, products, commerce, customs, etc.; all this valuable but obsolete information being crowded on the surface of the ten pip cards of the suit. The "J" (Jack) shows the principal islands which surround the continent; the "Q" (Queen) tells the quarter of the globe to which Africa belongs, with various statistics; and the "K" (King), the kingdoms or governments into which it is divided. The same formula is adopted on the other cards, — the Spades being devoted to Asia, the Hearts to Europe, and the Diamonds to America. Among the statements on the cards we find, on the Four of Diamonds: "The Dutch first planted colonies in New York, but these usurpers were obliged to own the right of the English to the land." On the "J" (Jack), among other islands mentioned, it states that "Long Island is 140 miles by 10. The middle is sandy. . . . The place called Lloyd's Neck, from its situation and fertility, is or might be made a paradise" (and this sentence probably led to the purchase and preservation of these precious cards). The chief towns of America and their

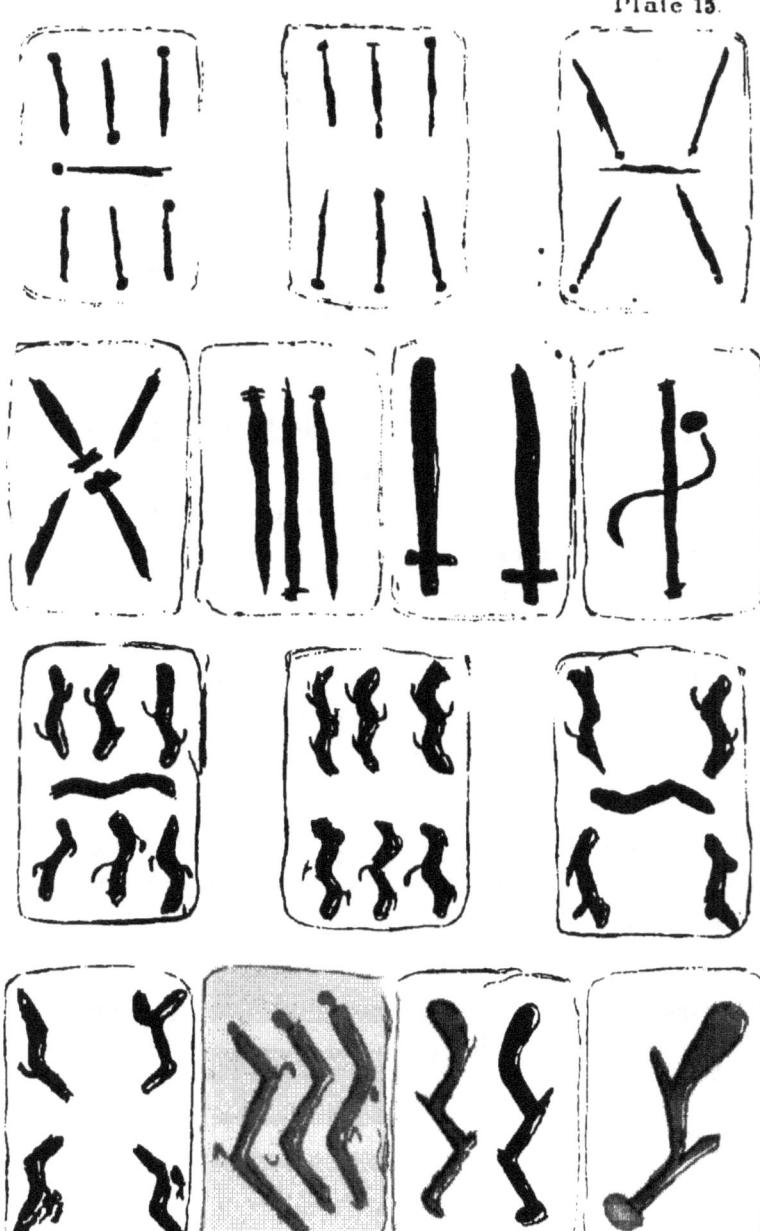

Plate 15.

population were given as follows : Mexico, 150,000 ; Lima, 60,000 ; Quito, 60,000 ; Cusco, 42,000 ; Panama and Philadelphia, 42,000 ; New York, 23,000 ; Boston, 19,000 ; Newport, 6,000.

What manner of game was played with these instructive cards is not now known. They were probably valued only as a book would have been which contained interesting information in a condensed form; and it is more than probable, from the excellent state of preservation in which they were found, that they were looked upon with awe by Miss Angelina, preserved with care, but never played with.

A letter from a sprightly young lady quoted in the "Republican Court," written during a visit to the Van Hornes of New York, which was probably about 1783, says: "All is a dead calm until the *cards* are introduced, when you see pleasure dancing in the eyes of all the matrons, and they seem to gain new life." But what were the favourite games of the dames of that city? She does not mention.

What has been called the national game of the United States, and the one at present in fashion among many classes of society, although perhaps not among the most refined and cultivated, is Poker. This game has its advocates, and a historiette of its own which is too widely known to require further comment here.

Among the terms used in playing it, and peculiar to it, are *blind*, which is supposed to have been derived from "bind;" *straddle*, which means to cover both the *blind* and the *ante*. The latter word may have been derived from the French *entrer*, to enter; as to *ante* is to enter the game by paying the stakes required.

Euchre, Commerce, Piquet, Bezique, and Whist are general favourites; and they have superseded the old-fashioned games of Brag (the father of Poker), Pope Joan, and others dear to the hearts of our grandmothers.

Among other ingenious means of evading the religious scruples that forbade playing-cards, some publisher hit upon the scheme of introducing to the public what he called "Yankee Notions." These were cards covered with distinctive symbols and marks of suits, and were accompanied by a small book of rules which has been embodied in an American edition of Hoyle for playing with them, and which contained the following preface:—

Plate 16.

"Believing that a settled prejudice exists with a large class of the community against the old-fashioned cards, the publisher has issued an entirely new style, to the introduction of which into every family circle there cannot possibly be the least objection. These cards and the games adapted to them are calculated to discipline and exercise the mind."

There are fifty cards in the pack, composed of five different suits; namely, Faces, Flags, Eagles, Stars, and Shields, "the honour cards being called the upper ten."

The directions for dealing, cutting, etc. are given, and are exactly the same as those in common use among all card-players, be they bent on gambling or only on innocent amusement.

The publisher goes on to state that "many things will serve for counters, as kernels of corn, or coffee, or old cards cut up. *For those who prefer something better the publisher of these cards has provided an ample supply at a small expense.*"

The difference between this pack and the ordinary cards generally played with seems to be only in the symbols which have been placed on them. The Flags, Eagles, etc., take the place of the Hearts,

Diamonds, Spades, and Clubs. To an unprejudiced mind the substitution of one symbol for another would not be sufficient to excuse the use of the "Yankee Notions" in places where ordinary playing-cards were regarded with disfavour. Sums of money might be as well staked and lost on Flags and Eagles as on Hearts and Diamonds, if the players were inclined to gamble on a game; and the term "to throw" or "to pass," which in the rules is employed instead of "to deal," might soothe the scruples of some minds, although the action in both cases were the same. That these games might be gambling, is proved by the suggestion about the counters.

The publisher of the "Yankee Notions" gives in his book of rules many games which could be played with his cards, one of which bears the ominous name of "Bunkum." Another game called "John Smith" is played under some droll rules. Among others is one which states that "the holder of Mrs. Smith, who is always anxious to recall her truant husband John to her side," must recite certain verses when she calls for him, "thinking him perhaps in doubtful company; and the position of John is one of *dread*, thinking he will be

Plate 17.

caught and possibly *Caudled*. The holder of Mrs. Smith will anxiously watch for the first opportunity to get the lead and call for her man John; for when she calls, John must go. She may say, —

> 'Come forth, great John,
> Thou paragon !
> My voice I 'm sure you know.'

He may reply, —

> ' I know that voice,
> I 've got no choice ;
> 'T is hard, but I must go.' "

The game resembles in many respects the kindred one of " Dr. Busby," in which the four suits contain only face and no pip cards. The suits being divided into four families, and the object of the game being to collect all the families in one hand by asking for each card by name from the right-hand neighbour, any mistake in naming over or "calling" for the cards causes the " call " to pass to the neighbour on the left, who then endeavours to ask for all the cards from the person who had been previously playing. This innocent game requires no counters, cannot possibly be used for gambling, and is an excellent exercise for the memory.

That cards were fashionable in some localities of the United States during the past century is proved not only by the invitations issued on the backs of playing-cards (of which specimens exist), and which have been already described, but also by the existence of numerous beautiful Japanese or Chinese lacquer counter-boxes which may be found any day carefully treasured in many families.

These boxes, which were originally imported especially for the person who ordered them, are usually of black and gold lacquer, oval in shape and covered with graceful arabesques of leaves and tendrils, which surround the initial letter of the owner's name, which was not only painted on the cover of the large box, but was also on each one of the tiny "fish boxes" contained inside of it. These strangely shaped little receptacles fitted compactly into the large boxes, and could be removed and replaced at pleasure. The centre of the box contained a number of small trays, especially designed for the favourite and at one time fashionable game of "Pope Joan." Each tray bore on its bottom a quaint figure painted in lacquer, which represented the Chinese idea of an ordinary court card; and this tray, according to the rules of the game, was to contain the counters when the players went through the customary formula and paid one to the Knave, two to the Queen, three to the King, four to the Ace, and five to "Pope Joan," which was represented by the *nine of Diamonds*. These convenient little trays were almost a necessity when playing this game; but substitutes were often ingeniously contrived by taking from an extra pack the necessary cards and bending their sides up until they would hold the counters without spilling them all over the table.

The counters, or "fish" (as our grandmothers called them), which were imported in these foreign boxes were made of small bits of mother of pearl which were of different sizes. Some of them were round, some oval, and some long, slender, and shaped somewhat like their namesakes the fish. They were usually engraved with quaint devices, a circular space being left in the centre of the counter intended to contain the initial letter of the owner's name, which was designed so as to match that placed on the boxes.

One set of counters in particular were imported by a naval officer for his family, and were small circular disks of pearl on which strange figures were painted in bright colours. These figures have become obliterated in the course of years. They came from their foreign home in a small round ivory box which contained only a limited number. They were always used for counters, but they may have been intended by the manufacturer for a game by themselves; and they somewhat resemble those described by Mr. Chatto, which he classed among the cards. Unfortunately nothing remains of the original pictures, and only a few dabs of colour now stain the tiny pearl disks, the outlines of the devices having been entirely obliterated.

Another most beautiful set of Chinese counters is contained in an ivory box. They are curiously carved with minute figures in low relief, and when first taken from their box were in regular order, and it seemed as if their pictured sides could relate a history. Unfortunately, the one hundred and sixty odd pieces soon became hopelessly mixed; and the tale they could have told was never related, and is now lost forever.

Besides the cards introduced into North America by Columbus and his sailors or by the emigrants to various parts of the country, strange

Plate 18.

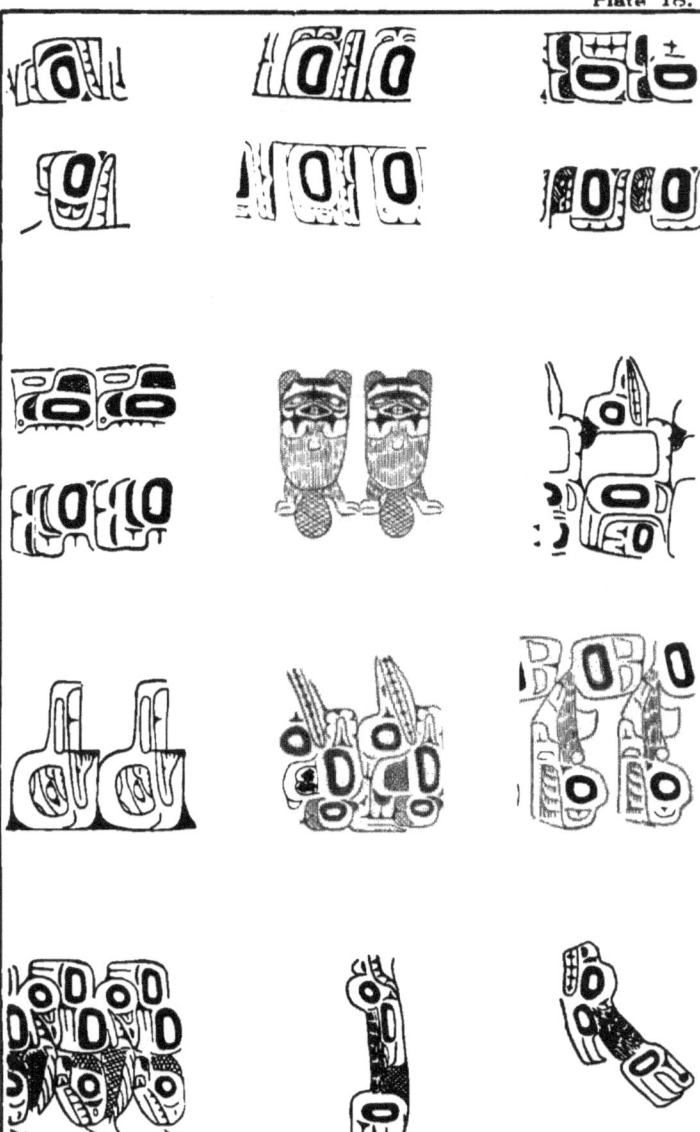

gambling instruments or sticks which may be called cards have been found among the Indians of southeastern Alaska and Queen Charlotte's Islands. These original and peculiar implements are made by the natives for their own use, and are of two kinds, — one set being beautifully carved with strange devices of birds, animals, men, etc.; the other set simply marked by lines of red or black paint rudely smeared on their rounded surface, but which are quite distinct enough to distinguish at a glance one from the other. The same game seems to be played with either the carved or painted set, although one seems to be only numbered, and the other to have no numbers and to rely on the carvings to represent the value of the stick.

From what source these Indians derived their "cards" will probably never be known. Taking into account the difference between card-board and cubes of wood, there is more than a fancied resemblance between these rude toys and the cards of Asia, and this may point to the original source. It is certain that they were not derived from the Spaniards or other emigrants who settled on the eastern coast of America and moved toward the west, as the emblems have nothing in common with European cards, whereas the cards used by the Apache Indians of Arizona show their derivation from the Spanish cards at once. These Indians make for themselves cards from deerskin, on which they paint in two colours — namely, red and blue — the *Oros, Denari, Espadas,* and *Copas* of the Spanish emblems. These deerskin cards are practically imperishable, as even the very rough usage which they undoubtedly have cannot destroy them; and they are greatly prized by their owners, who can seldom be induced to part with them. There are several packs of these cards in the National Museum at Washington, and one in the Museum at Boston.

A complete set of Haida gambling-sticks is also to be found in the National Museum; and casts of the carvings have been carefully taken on plaster, which displays the shape of the figures more plainly than the curved surfaces of the sticks can do. Thirty-two of these cubes compose "a pack," and these are contained in a leather pouch. The game is usually played by a number of persons, who squat on the ground in a circle around the dealer, who places the

Plate 19.

sticks in front of him under a pile of shavings or shredded cedar bark, and draws them out with great ceremony and hands them to the players, who receive them with grunts, cries, and other uncouth noises. Each stick has its value; and they are passed with great rapidity from one to the other, the players staking considerable amounts on the game.

These cubes are made of spruce, about six inches long and half an inch thick; on them patterns of birds, animals, fish, men, and other devices are cut. The designs necessarily adapt themselves to the curved surfaces, and on some are repeated, so that when the stick is held upright the same pattern is seen back to back. This arrangement is almost always followed, although there are exceptions to the rule. What the designs mean and what their value is no one seems to know, but it is quite evident that they are Tolemic devices; and these gambling-sticks are probably the most peculiar contrivances that have ever been invented to take the place of the pictured cards or the graven chessmen, and though not to be considered as a link between the two, certainly contain characteristics peculiar to both.

They may be classed into suits, which can be divided as follows: *Figures, Devices, Animals, Fish, Birds,* and *Reptiles* or *Insects.*

The suit of Figures has eight sticks. The first one is a man crowned, and holding in his right hand a fan, which seems to be a strange attribute when the climate of Queen Charlotte's Islands is considered. The carving on the second cube resembles that of a man seated, and leaning his chin on his hands, his elbows resting on his knees. Two semicircles over the head may represent a hat; fifteen notches placed on each side of this figure may show its value. Number three displays a seated figure, with what seems to be the soles of its feet turned outward; four circles cut beside the figure may denote its worth. The fourth cube represents a seated figure in profile, with one hand spread out to show the thumb and four fingers. This stick has no marks to denote its value, unless four notches deeply cut in its back may take their place. The fifth stick is an interesting one, as it seems intended to show both the face and back of the figure. Over the head are two semicircles resembling those on number two. The hands hang on each side, each

Plate 20.

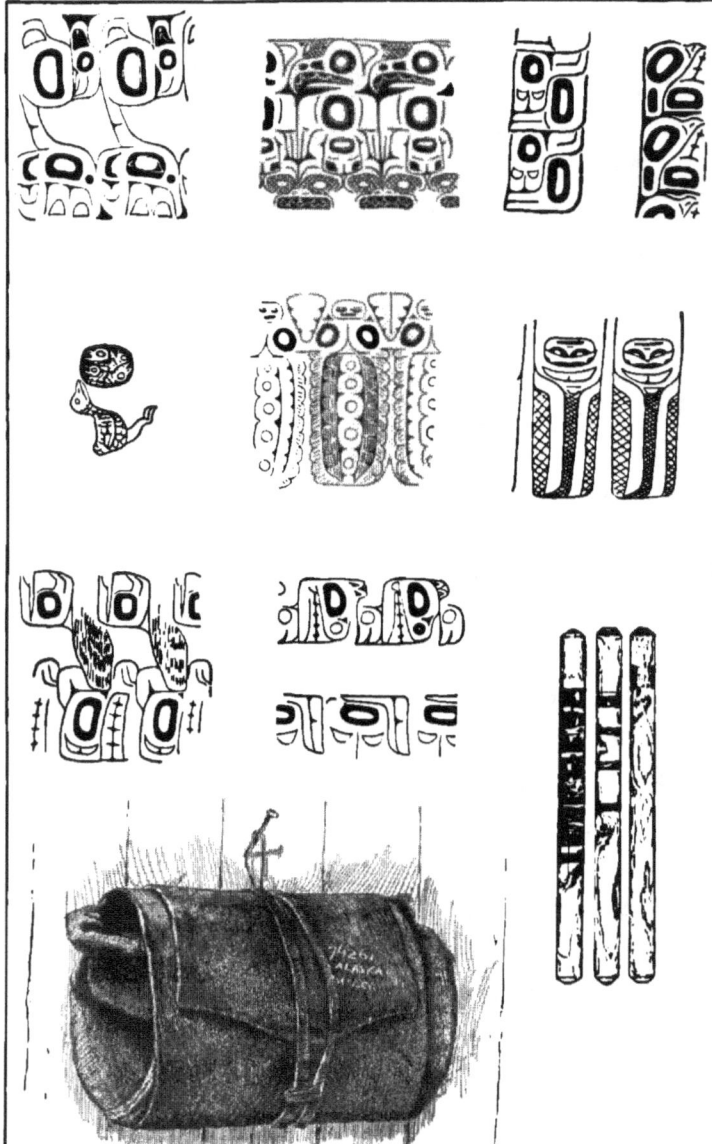

one having but three fingers and a thumb. The carvings on number six contain devices which resemble the lotus-flower. In a circle is a human face, the head surmounted by the semicircular cap. Number seven shows two grinning faces without bodies, but with arms and large hands displayed with the palms out. Two large chevrons divide these devices, which are cut across the stick, and not, as the others are, up and down its length. The eighth carving represents a hand with four well-shaped fingers and a thumb. Certain notches and cuts which surround the hand are undecipherable.

The eight succeeding cubes contain strange devices, which seem to represent fingers, eyes, teeth, etc., but which are confused and meaningless to the uninitiated. Number seventeen, on the contrary, shows a spirited and life-like carving of a beaver; and the next one a strange-looking monster, with a large mouth and huge teeth. The nineteenth cube has on it the head of some unrecognizable beast with a very long snout; and the twentieth, a ferocious-looking, large-mouthed animal. In cubes twenty-one, twenty-two, twenty-three, and twenty-four the carvings resemble fish;

twenty-two, in particular, shows a clever representation of a huge fish, and also a duck. Twenty-five, twenty-six, twenty-seven, and twenty-eight call to mind birds; the twenty-sixth cube, in particular, showing most plainly the head, wings, and claws of what may be intended for an eagle. The stick which is numbered twenty-eight has on it a carving of a bird perched beside a nest which contains four fledglings.

The last four sticks are as well carved and deeply cut as any of the others in the pack, number twenty-nine bearing a spirited cut of a beetle; but the others cannot be as easily deciphered. The carvings of the beaver, the eagle, and the beetle represent these creatures in an erect or upright attitude, instead of the one natural to the animal. Whether this has some peculiar significance or not remains to be proved.

The "gambling-sticks" used by the Alaska Indians closely resemble those already described; and they also have two kinds of "sticks," some of them carved and some painted. There are fifty-four cubes in the painted pack, some of them perfectly plain or unpainted; two more plain sticks have notched ends, which probably

Plate 21.

increases their value. Fourteen of the sticks have stripes painted on them, but these are so faint and blurred as to be almost unnoticeable. None of this set are notched. Three sticks are striped with black bars, one, two, and three in number; five sticks have red bands. Another set of six sticks have red and black stripes, numbering from one to eight. All these sticks are notched at one end, and, besides the bars, have on them smears of red or black paint. The game played with the painted sticks appears to be the same as that played with the carved ones; and the former are also kept in a leather pouch, which is bound or tied with a leather thong.

JAPAN.

IT is to Japan that we must turn when we wish to find the most dainty and original of Playing-cards. This interesting nation have devised for themselves the symbols that they use, which are so unique that they bear no features in common with those of any other country, if we except one device which may be an accidental one, and which will hereafter be mentioned; otherwise the Japanese playing-cards differ completely from those of other places, except that they are painted on pasteboard and highly glazed or varnished.

Those writers who trace in European and other cards a resemblance to the classes of society into which the world is divided, and promulgate the opinion that the four suits commonly seen represent them, — namely, the Cup or Priest, the Sword or Soldier, Money the Merchant, and Maces the Artisan, — would find it impossible to divide the Japanese cards in this way, as they belong distinctly to a new set of ideas, and seem to have been originated in the Islands, where alone they are used, and do not show, as those of other nations do, some mark or device which betrays to the student an inherited symbol which may be traced to the original Oriental card.

Japanese cards are of the same shape as those used by the French and other European nations, but are very much smaller than ordinary cards, being a little more than two inches long by one broad. They are made of pasteboard, on the back of which black paper has been carefully pasted over the edges of the cards so as to leave a narrow rim to form a frame on the face of the

Plate 22.

card. The symbols are stencilled, and the whole card varnished or enamelled, so that they are extremely slippery.

Forty-nine in number, they are divided into twelve suits of four each, with one card which is a trifle smaller than the others, and which has a plain white face and is used as a "Joker." On the other cards are painted flowers or emblems appropriate to the twelve months of the year; each card is distinct and different from its fellows, even when bearing the same emblem, and they can be easily distinguished and classified not only by the design they bear, but also by a character or letter which marks nearly every card, and which seems to denote the vegetable that represents the month.

January is marked by pine-trees, two of the cards showing them against a lurid sky. On the third the pine stands out on a grayish background; and the fourth has a setting sun flecked with light clouds, the pines barely indicated in front of it, and the larger part of the card being covered with the figure of a white-bodied, red-eyed stork. February displays as her emblem a plum-blossom; the four cards devoted to the month bearing the flower in various positions. March has a red cherry-blossom, and April the hanging tendrils of the wisteria vine; and on one of the cards belonging to this month there is a wee yellow-bird which is flying across its surface under a red cloud. For May there are four beautiful blue irises, with long spiky leaves; one card showing in its corner part of a dock and the water, from which the flower is lifting its lovely head. June is represented by blood-red peonies, one of the cards having two yellow butterflies hovering over the flowers. On July's cards star-shaped leaves, some yellow, some red, and some black, are scattered over their surfaces. These leaves resemble those of the maple-trees. On one of the cards belonging to this July suit a deer stands under the branches of this tree; and it is this deer that is the one device which may be found on cards belonging to other nations. Some packs of Chinese cards have deer on one of their cards, and in ancient Spanish packs animals resembling deer can be seen, although they are usually represented with one straight horn something like a unicorn, which fabulous animal has been retained in Spanish cards to this day.

Plate 23.

August has four pictures of grass-covered mountains. In three of them there is a cloudy blue sky, and the fourth shows the sun looking hot and sultry, beaming down on the treeless elevation. Three birds fly across the sky on one of these cards. September bears the Mikado's flower,— a party-coloured yellow and red chrysanthemum; October a "Hägi" with red or green leaves, and on one card is a yellow boar trotting along under the spreading branches of the tree.

November shows on one card willow-trees sharply defined against a leaden sky. The willows on the fellow cards look wind-tossed, and a long-tailed bird skims across the sky. A third card is covered with inky clouds and torrents of rain, with strange zigzags shooting over its surface looking like forked lightning. The fourth card of this suit bears the quaint figure of a man rushing under the willow-trees through the storm and dropping his sandals in his haste, his head covered by a huge yellow umbrella and surrounded by streaks of lightning, with the rain streaming down on his unprotected body.

December carries the Imperial Japanese plant,

Kiri; and over one of the flowers hovers a beautiful red-crested pheasant with silver wings.

The chrysanthemum is the Mikado's plant, and the Kiri the national flower of Japan. The favourite game at present seems to be like Casino, in which any card of a set can take up any other card, but each one has a particular value in the final count. An infinite variety of games may be played with these cards, as there is a shade of difference in each one, and to the accustomed eye they are as easy to sort as the European ones. There is a great difference in the style and finish of Japanese cards. Some of them are carefully executed and highly varnished; but other packs are roughly stencilled and show but little glaze. The "Joker" is not necessarily part of the pack, and does not accompany each one.

Plate 24

THE KING.

THE KING.

> "Behold four Kings in majesty rever'd
> With hoary whiskers and a forky beard.
> . . . . . .
> The hoary Majesty of Spades appears,
> Puts forth one manly leg to sight revealed,
> The rest in many-coloured robe concealed."

EVEN Pope in his description of the game of Ombre has thought it not beneath his notice to describe the appearance of the monarchs of the cards; indeed theirs is no uninteresting history, and although but slightly alluded to by the chroniclers of their day, they have many a time played quite as important a part and had as much influence in their way as the monarch who was seated on a more stable throne than a paper one, and who sometimes himself yielded to the fascinations of his rival of cards.

That the dress worn by the Kings in the English court cards is a rude copy of that of the notorious Henry the Eighth of England is not only a matter of tradition, but is also supported by a reference to the existing portraits of that monarch.

Notwithstanding the fact that the crowns of the card Kings are "*fleurdelisés*," which seems to point at first to a French origin, the dress in other respects bears a close resemblance to that of bluff King Harry.

In French and German packs the Kings generally bear sceptres, globes, and other insignia of their exalted rank; but those of the English cards are warriors to the core, and throwing aside the emblems, which only show their rank, they arm themselves and stand ready for the fray. Their Majesties of Spades, Clubs, and Hearts hold up their trusty double-edged swords like the brave men that they are; the King of Hearts being in a most warlike attitude, with his uplifted sword held ready for a blow. The King of Spades alone carries a battle-axe; but why he in particular adopted this weapon in preference to any other, history does not declare.

Among the French packs the royal family are always distinguished by names which are plainly written on some part of the card; and these names vary according to the date of the pack, and seemingly through the caprice of the card-maker. French authors have traced the origin of these names to various celebrated personages, and find that they were assumed to do honour to the reigning monarchs of the period, their queens or mistresses, or some favourite hero of the hour, either real or fictitious; and the only limit to the variety of these names was the imagination of the designer.

A glance over any old collection of French cards will verify this assertion; but the fashion does not seem to have been followed in other countries, even in England, where the symbols of the French were adopted in preference to those used in Spain, Germany, and other places. Their Majesties of Cards were not dubbed with names, and if originally intended to represent some particular person (as some of them, notably the Kings and Queens, undoubtedly were), the names were not placed on the cards, and we have only tradition on which to rest the presumption that they were intended for any celebrated character either in history or fiction.

To return to the French cards, those for example which are supposed to have been made for Charles the Seventh bear no inscriptions but that of the maker's name; but in a nearly contemporaneous pack the King of Diamonds is named *Corsube*, the King of Clubs *Sans Souci*, and he of Spades *Apollin*. This collection of names, says one writer, shows a triple influence,— the Eastern origin of the cards, in the first place, as they bear strange cognomens which are not French; in the second, the impression that the old romances of chivalry had made on the mind of the designer; and third, the reflection in them of contemporaneous events.

Many persons point to this pack as being the very one that was designed by Étienne Vignoles, or, as he was usually called, La Hire, or Chevalier, and declare that they are the oldest examples that bear the symbols of Hearts, Diamonds, Clubs, and Spades. Going back to the names borne by the card Kings, we fancy that we see that the one assumed by his Majesty of Spades (Apollin) was derived from that borne by an idol adored by the Saracens, which is mentioned in an epic poem of the period; and Corsube was a knight of Cordue (Corsuba), who was glorified by the romancers of that day. The names of the Queens and Knaves of this pack are those of celebrated historical characters.

Another old pack which belongs without doubt to the reign of Louis the Twelfth contains a King of Hearts named Charles, a King of Diamonds Cæsar, one of Clubs Artus, and of Spades David; and in a later one belonging to the commencement of the reign of Francis the First the King of Clubs has become Alexander.

About the time of the battle of Pavia and the captivity of the French King (Francis) in Spain and his marriage with the dowager Eleanor, the influence of Spanish and also of Italian fashions shows itself in many ways in the cards, and the names of the Kings are changed to Julius Cæsar, Charles, Hector, and David.

Under the reign of Henry the Second the names bestowed upon the cardboard sovereigns begin to resemble those borne by them in the French pack of the present day. The King of Diamonds is Cæsar; of Spades, David; and of Clubs, Alexander.

During the period when Henry the Third governed France the cards became the reflectors of the extravagant fashions of that effeminate reign. The Kings in card-land wore pointed beards, like the reigning monarch; their collars, like his, were stiffly starched; they had hats bearing long plumes, and their breeches were puffed out at the hips in a most extraordinary way; while, as if to make the figure look as slender and as womanly as possible, the doublet was pinched in at the waist; and they had peculiar boots, which were then the mode.

Henry the Fourth mounted the throne of France, and the card Kings immediately altered their costumes and their names, and reflected the aspect of his court, and the names of the heroes of the day were given to the gentlemen of the card circle.

The paper sovereigns generally mirrored the characteristics of the day; and when the successors of Henry the Fourth mounted the throne the change is at once shown in the cards, either by the names, the dresses, the weapons, or by all these. At one time Italian fashions and customs, imported by Marie de' Medici, influenced them, and the names became Carel, Capet, Melun, etc.; and they change with amusing rapidity after her death.

A most interesting and almost boundless field of research opens before the student who wishes to trace in these seemingly meaningless variations the prominent events and fashions of the period, which are stamped on the cards, and can be easily traced. This has induced many persons to make elaborate studies from them; and one in particular, Père Daniel, declares that he can detect the fact that *David*, one of the original names of the King of Spades, is intended to represent Charles the Seventh of France; and he draws an elaborate parallel between the character of the real king and the characteristics of the mimic one as represented on the cardboard. Other authors demur at this, but it is at least worthy of note.

During the time of the French Revolution it was not only the royal family who were deposed and beheaded; but the same fate also followed their Majesties of Spades, Clubs, Diamonds, and Hearts.

"The King was slyly fingered from the deck;"

the sovereigns were banished, and their places supplied by pictured representations of sages and philosophers. The Reign of Reason did not last long; and the royal family were recalled in 1813, and established more firmly than ever on their ancient thrones, from whence even the republican *cartiers* of the present day in France have not desired to depose them, to replace their serene highnesses with presidents, senators, and other rulers of the revised republic.

Some attempts have been made in the United States of America to supplant the kings in their government of the card world, by placing the pictures of prominent generals in their place; and after the triumphant termination of the war with Mexico in 1848 a pack was issued on which Generals Scott, Bragg, Wool, and Twiggs took the place of the sovereigns of the packs as rulers of the card suits. But these peculiar cards, handsome as they were in their details, did not meet with popular favour, and are only found in some collections, while the " Great Republic " meekly bows its head, and submits to the dominion of the Kings of Diamonds, of Hearts, of Clubs, and of Spades, who rule triumphantly over it as well as the greater part of the civilized world, dressed, as they have been for hundreds of years, like their brother Henry the Eighth of England; and every deviation from this quaint garb is frowned down at once by their loyal subjects, who detest all changes in card-land, and cling to the obsolete costumes and quaint figures with unswerving loyalty.

It is worth while to note the interesting fact that the first sovereigns of the French cards are still in existence, and are now preserved in Paris in the Cabinet des Estampes. These are the cards which have already been mentioned as having been the identical ones invented for the amusement of Charles the Seventh by one of his courtiers. That they are the same is not doubted by any authorities.

The names of the Kings of this pack — Corsube, Apollon, etc. — have already been dwelt upon, and their probable origin traced. They are minutely described by Mr. Taylor in his " History of Cards," who says: " The figures are engraved on wood, printed with a pale ink of a brownish tint, and afterwards coloured with stencil in the usual manner. The crowns of the kings are formed of fleurs-de-lis, and the costumes are those of the period of Charles the Seventh."

These cards were discovered in Lyons by a

M. Henin, who found them pasted in the cover of a book of the fifteenth century, of which they formed part of the binding. Their fortunate discoverer well understood the value of this prize, and they were carefully removed, and are now treasured as the first specimens of cards which were divided into suits with the symbols which they now bear. The bookbinder's knife has shaved off the title of the King of Hearts, or rather his name; otherwise the principal court cards are almost uninjured, and are preserved with the respect they deserve to have as the oldest surviving monarchs of the world, — their age being nearly five hundred years, the date of their invention being about 1425.

THE QUEEN.

THE QUEEN.

AS we turn to study "the Little Madames of the Would-be family," as the Queens of the cards have been called, mention must first be made of their creation.

It seems impolite to note and dwell upon a lady's age, however great it may be; but the birth of the first Queen of cards marks an epoch and is worth recording, notwithstanding the fact that it took place as far back in the history of the world as 1425. At this date, as has been mentioned, the cards were first separated from the original Tarots and divided into suits, which were distinguished by the symbols that they now bear in France; and the old devices which resembled money, swords, and other strange designs were discarded. The figures on the cards were also changed, and the Vizir was discarded and disappeared with the old marks which distinguished the suits.

Their Majesties the first Queens of cards are, with their royal consorts, preserved in the French

Museum. The history of their invention has already been related. The Adams of the pack were, by the politeness of the French courtier, provided with Eves, and they have become the ancestors of countless millions of successors.

Previous to the arrangement of the Tarot cards into the more convenient pack which is now generally used, the female figure was placed in that part of the pack which was divided into suits, although among the twenty-two emblematical cards named Atouts were found an Empress, and Pope Joan, and other female figures representing justice, temperance, etc. In some packs of Tarots the Queens joined the male figures; but their presence is not common, and these packs were comparatively modern. In the place now occupied by the Queen there was a Cavalier, Knight, General, Vizir, or whatever might have been the name of the male figure which was second in rank in card-land, and he had the Queen's place and value. This was the descendant of the same warrior who in the ancient games of Chess was placed beside the King; and the position which that piece occupied was much more in accordance with the energy, the strategy, and the manœuvring to be looked for in a marshal in command of an army, than from the wife of a reigning sovereign.

Mr. Chatto states that at an early period the Italians occasionally substituted a Queen for the Cavello, and declares that the French have claimed an honour which does not belong to them when they assert that they were the first nation that had the gallantry to place a lady in the pack.

This example, set by the French or perhaps by the Italians, of placing a queen among the court cards has not been followed by other nations, nor indeed to any very great extent by the Italians themselves, who, although they sometimes included her, only do so, as a general rule, when they adopt the French cards and their symbols entirely, and discard those derived from the East, which have been clung to since their first introduction.

England was one of the few nations gallant enough to retain the lady in the national pack when it had emigrated from France and taken root in its adopted country; and England also selected a particular Queen of her own, and placed her figure among the court cards.

In one of the pictures of Elizabeth of York,

wife of Henry the Seventh of England, we find the original of the quaint dress now worn by our cardboard queens. There were various reasons for the selection of this lady and her elevation to the paper throne, where she has remained, with her costume and even the colour of her hair almost unchanged, to the present day, and which a cursory examination of her history will reveal. During the lifetime of her father Edward the Fourth of England, Elizabeth was betrothed to the dauphin Charles, eldest son of Louis the Eleventh of France. At that time there was constant intercourse with the sister country, and cards may then have been first imported into England. The English princess after her contract with the heir of France was always addressed as Madame la Dauphine, and her picture may have been placed on the cards to show that she took rank as a French princess. This match was, however, suddenly terminated by the French monarch, and his rage and disappointment it is said caused her father's death. Her marriage with his successor, which joined the two houses of York and Lancaster, who had been rival claimants for the throne of England, terminated forever the Wars of the Roses; and it may have been during the period of great rejoicing which followed this auspicious event that the royal dame who had been elevated to the position of Queen Consort was also selected to reign over card-land, where her figure, dress, and attributes are cherished to this day.

If we turn to the picture of Elizabeth of York, we shall see at a glance where the card-maker derived his inspiration for the costume of the card Queens. Over the heads of the royal dames are odd-looking head-dresses, which in the lapse of years have become rigidly conventionalized; but in them can easily be traced the resemblance to the straight lappets made of a scarf or veil richly embroidered with jewels, forming a cap and hanging on either side of the face, which forms part of the dress in the picture of Elizabeth. In it her hair, which was of a pale golden hue, is banded plainly on her forehead, and she wears a square-cut dress, which opens at her throat and has long flowing ermine-edged sleeves. One of the most important parts of the picture must be carefully noted. The Queen holds the rose of York in her hand, and this emblem has been always copied and retained.

Elizabeth of York was a most beautiful woman, and it might have been due to this fact that her picture was so eagerly copied. She died very young, having only attained her thirty-eighth year, in 1503, leaving an heir to the throne, who was afterward Henry the Eighth.

Among the names bestowed upon the Queens of the French court cards are those of Hélène, Judic, Rachael. These are found in the pack which is believed to be of the time of Louis the Twelfth. When the war with Spain took place, which was followed by the capture and imprisonment of Francis the First and his marriage with the Queen Eleanor, the ladies of the pack change their names to Lucresse, Pentaxlie, Beciabia. Again, under the reign of Henry the Second they become Argine, Pallas, etc. The effeminate reign of Henry the Third affected the dresses as well as the names on the cards. The Queens wore their hair turned back and crepé, "la robe juste à corps et a vertu garde," and bear such names as Dido, Elizabeth, and Clotilde.

Singer relates that Pallas, as the Queen of Spades was at one time named, was intended to represent Joan of Arc, the Maid of Orleans, as

Pallas was goddess of war and of chastity, and the Maid was her worthy representative; and that Charles the Seventh, out of gratitude for the services received at her hands, caused her to be placed under the cover of the heathen goddess's name in card-land.

Père Daniel, in his dissertation on the "Game of Piquet," says that the Queen of Clubs is called *Argine*, from which the anagram Regina may be made, and that it is intended to represent Marie d'Anjou, wife of Charles the Seventh. Rachael was chosen to represent Agnes Sorel, whose token — the clover-leaf (*sorel*) — was placed among the symbols of the suits. The same author fancies that Judith may be intended to represent Isabel of Bavaria, mother of Charles the Seventh and wife of Charles the Sixth.

THE KNAVE.

THE KNAVE.

THE Knave has always been given an original and sometimes a prominent place in the pack of cards. Although this position does not seem to have been derived directly from *Il Matto*, or the *Fool* of the Tarots, he seems to have inherited some of the peculiarities of the latter; and in many games he is given the same position, and either takes precedence of all the other court cards or else adds to their value according to the rules of the particular game which is being played.

The word "knave" in the English language was originally used to signify a "boy." Chaucer employs it in this sense where he says of the King of Northumberland, —

"On hire he gat a knave child;"

and this name was given by the English to the card which was called by the French *le Valet*, as they regarded the male figure which accompanied the court cards on their invasion of their country as the son of the King and Queen of the suit to which he belonged, and did not recognize his position as the court-jester or servant of the royal family. But the words " man-child " or "knave" used in the sense of "boy" soon became obsolete, and the latter is never seen in the present day except to denote a cheat, dishonest person, or the second male figure of the court cards.

To the same card is frequently given the name *Jack*. It is supposed that this name was derived from the party-coloured or buffoon's dress worn by the Knave; the cant name for a jester being "Jack," which was also the term used to designate a serving-man of low degree. The expression "Jack-a-napes" was probably derived from "Jack-a-Naïpes," or Jack of the cards, *Naïpes* being the Spanish name for the pack; and as cards were at one time imported into England quite as much from Spain as from France, it was usual to call them by the Spanish as well as the French name. Mr. Chatto declares that "Jack-a-napes" means "Jack the Knave," and says that "this card has more affinity in character with the Spanish *Sota* or the Italian *Faute* than with the French *Valet;*" and he also says: " We believe that it has never been explained why the coarse and vulgar appellation of Knave was originally given to the card next in degree to the Queen. Perhaps the following account may be found a plausible one. It was usual with kings in ancient times to choose some ludicrous person with whose ridiculous and comical tricks they might be diverted in their hours of ease. This person was generally selected from the lower ranks; but choice always fell on one endowed with low cunning and humour calculated to excite mirth and laughter; and the tricks of knavery in which he was allowed free indulgence in the presence of the King gave him the appellation of King's Fool, or Knave."

In the German pack the Knave has been called *Lansknechte* (Free Lancer), and from this has been derived the name of a well-known game which the French call "Lansquenet." In early French packs the same card was sometimes termed *Trichem*, which was also the name of a formidable band of robbers who at one time committed such horrible ravages in France that the Popes were obliged to preach a crusade against them.

The grotesque dress of the Knaves of the English packs has remained almost unchanged for several hundred years. It has evidently been copied from the ordinary costumes of the fifteenth or sixteenth centuries, but no exact date can be assigned to it. It seems to consist of a short jacket with full flowing sleeves, the body being crossed by a sash, or what may have originally been intended for a strap to hold a quiver. This coat, or jacket, resembles the *gaberdine* described by Chaucer as being the dress of the Squires in the "Canterbury Tales." The cap, with its squarely cut or battlemented edges, turned back over an under-cap of black, which fitted closely to the head, was in common use about the end of the fifteenth century. The Knaves of to-day are cut in halves, and show two heads, which are legless; and these replace the old standing figures and the odd-looking, misshapen, party-coloured legs, which followed an ancient fashion, and showed one clothed in one colour, its fellow being dressed in a different one, with gayly striped garters and peculiarly shaped shoes.

Mr. Taylor tells a droll story, which shows how conservative people have for many years been on the subject of cards, and how they resent the smallest change in the costume, etc., of the court cards, when every other dress changes almost as soon as it is generally adopted. He says: "One of the large card-makers in London many years ago introduced a scarcely perceptible modification in the colour of the Knave's garter. Cards were supplied, as usual, to the customers; but very soon the steward of one of the considerable clubs came rushing down in a great hurry to the shop. 'The committee can't think what you have been doing to the cards! All the members are complaining that they keep losing. What have you done?' At first the card-maker said, 'Done? Why, nothing!' not thinking the trifling change of any importance; but on further inquiry it was found that the indescribable something the clubbists had detected confused them, and he was obliged to take back all his cards and supply those of the former sort. Such is the influence of a trifle. Since that time, however, many alterations have been introduced, and not a few improvements."

The weapons which are placed in the hands of the Knaves have become strangely distorted with the lapse of time and through the carelessness of the card-maker. Our Knave of Hearts bears a clumsy-looking battle-axe, which looks too dull and too heavy to be of much service in case of necessity; and in the other hand he holds a laurel leaf. The Knave of Diamonds has what Falstaff calls a "Welsh hook," which has been defined as meaning "a pike with a hook placed at some distance below its point." The peculiar attribute of the present Knave of Spades is a twisted ribbon, and its origin has not been traced. It may originally have been a Marotte, or Fool's Staff, around which gayly coloured ribbons were twisted, the whole surmounted with a fool's cap. This Knave formerly bore a strange-looking instrument; but its use having become obsolete, even its form has been discarded, and the figure bears no weapon of defence, like his confrères. The strange-looking staff carried by the Knave of Clubs is supposed to have been originally intended for an arrow.

Why it is that the Knaves of Hearts and Spades should be in profile, while the others show their full face, will probably always remain a mystery; but it may be observed that the Knave of Hearts is in the same position in some very old packs, now preserved in the British Museum, to which has been attributed the date of 1440; and the same thing occurs in a picture which is prefixed to a book called "The Four Knaves," which was published in 1613.

As has been before mentioned, the court cards of the French packs have always had names placed somewhere on the face of the card; and these names, after changing with some rapidity with the fashions of the day, have now become permanent, and for some years have been retained without the slightest variation. "Hector," as one of the Knights is dubbed, is supposed to recall Hector de Galard, Captain of the Guard, to Louis the Eleventh of France. Some authors think that Hector, the son of Priam, is intended by this name, as on some old cards the inscription is "Hector de Troye." Another Knave bears the name of "Roland," which was that of a nephew of Charlemagne. "Hogier," or Ogier, was a renowned King of Denmark. Lancelot may have at first been intended as a compliment for a Paladin of the court of Charlemagne, who was a celebrated character of his day; or perhaps Lancelot du Lac, as it was sometimes written, may have been intended for one of the Knights of King Arthur's Round Table. La Hire, another name placed beside the

Knaves, was that of the celebrated Étienne de Vignolles, who contributed so much by his valour to re-establish the tottering throne of Charles the Seventh of France. Mr. Singer says that he was surnamed La Hire. Some authors attribute the arrangement of the French pack, with the symbols of the Hearts, Diamonds, Clubs, and Spades, and the black and red colours, to the same La Hire.

ACES AND OTHER CARDS.

ACES AND OTHER CARDS.

IT would seem that the name *ace*, *as*, *asso*, or at any rate some combination of letters which convey about the same sound, is given to the first card in the pack in nearly all countries where they are used. Mr. Chatto says, according to Père Daniel, the Ace is the Latin *as*, meaning "a piece of money, coin, riches;" while Bullet derives it from the Celtic, and says that it means "origin, source, beginning, or first." A French writer of the sixteenth century, supposed to be Charles Stephens, in a work entitled "Paradoxes," printed at Paris, 1553, says that the "Ace or Az ought to be called *Nars*, a word which in German signifies a 'fool.'" The German word which he alludes to, continues Mr. Chatto, "is just as likely to have been the origin of Deuce as of Ace. It has also been supposed that the term 'ace' was derived from a Greek word signifying 'one.' But as this also signified an 'ass,' it has been conjectured that the Ace of Cards and of Dice were so called not as a designation of unity, but as signifying an ass or a fool. Those who entertain the latter opinion are said by Hyde to be asses themselves."

Aces have had soubriquets or nicknames like many other cards; but these have gained favour only in certain localities. In one part of England they are called *Tib;* but the origin and meaning of this name is unknown. The Ace of Diamonds is commonly called the *Earl of Cork* in Ireland, "because it is the worst Ace and the poorest card in the pack, and he is the poorest nobleman in the country." In Spain the Ace of Oros is called *La Borgne,* or the "one-eyed."

"There is luck under a black Deuce," is a common saying among card-players. "But not if you touch it with your elbow," is the reply; and when it is turned up as a trump, superstitious people place their elbow upon it, and quite a struggle goes on between the dealer and the opponent as to which one shall do so first. It is more than probable that the words *Deuce* and *Tray* may have been derived from the Spanish *Dos* and *Tres*, which signify "two" and "three" in that language. In some

German games the *Daus* is the master card, and takes all the others. Mr. Chatto says: " The Deuce of cards, it may be observed, has no connection with the term *deuce*, as used in the familiar expression 'To play the deuce,' in which it is synonymous with *devil*, and is of northern origin. In some parts of the country the Deuce, although lower in value, is considered to be a more fortunate card than the Tray; and 'There's luck in the Deuce, but none in the Tray,' is a frequent expression among old card-players who like to enliven the game with an occasional remark as they lay down the cards."

In Northumberland, England, the four of Hearts at Whist is sometimes called *Hob Collingwood*, and is considered by old ladies an unlucky card. The four of Clubs is called by sailors *the Devil's Bedposts*, and the four of Spades is named by others *Ned Stokes*. The Tray of Oros, in Spain, is called *Le Seigneur*. The Tray of Cups is *La Dame;* the Deuce is *La Vache*. The nines of Cups and of Money are the *Great and Little Nines*, and the Ace of Clubs is *Le Serpent*. In Ireland the six of Hearts is known as *Grace's Card*, and is said to have acquired that name from the following circumstance: "A gentleman of the name of Grace being solicited with promises of royal favour to espouse the cause of William the Third, gave the following answer written on the back of the six of Hearts, to an emissary of Marshal Schomberg, who had been commissioned to make the offer to him: 'Tell your master I despise his offer, and that honour and conscience are dearer to a gentleman than all the wealth and titles a prince can bestow.'"

"The nine of Diamonds," continues Mr. Chatto, "is frequently called the *Curse of Scotland*, and some suppose on account of the tradition that the Duke of Cumberland wrote his sanguinary order on it after the battle of Culloden. It was, however, known by this name many years before this battle, as it is stated that about 1715 Lord Justice Clerk Ormistone, who had been zealous in suppressing the rebellion became universally hated in Scotland, where they called him 'the curse of Scotland;' and when ladies played the nine of Diamonds (commonly called the Curse of Scotland), they called it Justice Clark." Other explanations are offered to account for this name, some of them being found in heraldic devices, as nine diamonds or lozenges are displayed in the arms of various distinguished men notorious for their hatred and persecution of that country. The riddle on the subject says: "*Question.* Pray why is the nine of Diamonds called the Curse of Scotland? *Answer.* Because the crown of Scotland had but nine diamonds in it, and they were never able to get a tenth." The nine of Diamonds is the card designated to represent Pope Joan in the game known by her name. The fours have been called *Tidely*, and the fives and sixes *Towser* and *Tumbler*.

The court cards have not escaped these soubriquets. In France the Knaves or Valets were sometimes called *les Fous*, and in Germany the horsemen or chevaliers who took the place of the Queens were designated *Ober*. In certain games the Knave of Clubs is called *Pam;* and in Euchre Knaves are called *Right* and *Left Bower*, as they happen to fall with trumps. The Queen of Clubs has been called *Queen Bess*.

It is mentioned in "Court Life below Stairs," by Molloy, as a curious feature of the time, and showing how far presumptuous gamblers forgot their manners and their loyalty, that during one of the attacks of lunacy suffered by the King, George the Third, great abuse of the King and Queen, and of Pitt was indulged in without reserve at Brook's Club; and a cant phrase used at the whist-table was, "I play the lunatic," meaning the King.

USE AND ABUSE.

USE AND ABUSE.

STRANGE tales have been related of the various uses to which cards have been put, and Mr. Singer tells one of a Friar " who, thinking to pull out his Breviary, displays a pack of cards which some mischievous wit had substituted for it. Not at all disconcerted by the circumstance, he explains to the people that he makes use of them as a Breviary, and in a most ingenious manner applies the different cards to this purpose."

There is another history of a parson who loved gaming better than his eyes, quoted by Mr. Chatto. This preacher thrust his cards up his sleeves when the clerk called him to the pulpit. " 'T is true that in the height of his reproving his parish for their neglect of holy duties, upon the throwing out of his zealous arm, the cards dropped out of his sleeve and flew about the church. What then? He bid one boy take up a card, and asked him what it was. The boy answers, 'The King of Clubs.' Then he bid another boy take up another card. What was that? 'The Knave of Spades.' 'Well,' quoth he, 'now tell me who made ye?' The boy could not well tell. Quoth he to the next, 'Who redeemed ye?' That was a harder question. 'Look ye,' quoth the parson, 'you think this was an accident, and laugh at it; but I did it on purpose to show you that had you taught your children their catechism as well as to know their cards, they would have been better provided to answer material questions when they come to church.'"

The story does not. go on to state that this precious preacher met the fate of Ananias, as he well deserved to do.

Not many years ago in England, the following story printed on a sheet or pamphlet, was circulated among the poorer classes and was received with great favour. It was called : " Cards Spiritualized ; or the Soldier's Almanac, Bible, and Prayer-Book."

Richard Middleton, a soldier attending divine service with the rest of a regiment at a church in Glasgow, instead of pulling out a Bible like the rest of his fellow soldiers to find the parson's text, spread a pack of cards before him. This singular behaviour did not long pass unnoticed both by the clergyman and the sergeant of the company to which he belonged. The latter, in particular, requested him to put up the cards, and on his refusing, conducted him after church before the mayor, to whom he preferred a formal complaint of Richard's indecent behaviour during divine service.

"Well, soldier," said the mayor, "what excuse have you for this strange, scandalous behaviour? If you can make any apology or assign any reason for it; it is well; if you cannot, assure yourself that I will cause you without delay to be severely punished for it."

"Since your Honour is so good," replied Richard, "I will inform you. I have been eight days on march, with a bare allowance of sixpence a day, which your Honour will surely allow is hardly sufficient to maintain a man in meat, drink, washing, and other necessaries that consequently he may want, without a Bible, Prayer-Book, or any other good book." On saying this, Richard drew out his pack of cards, and presenting one of the Aces to the mayor continued his address to the magistrate as follows:—

"When I see an Ace, may it please your Honour, it reminds me that there is only one God; and when I look upon a two or a three, the former puts me in mind of the Father and Son, and the latter of the Father, Son, and Holy Ghost. A four calls for remembrance the four evangelists, Matthew, Mark, Luke, and John. A five, the five wise Virgins who were ordered to trim their lamps. There were ten indeed; but five, your Worship may remember, were wise and five were foolish. A six, that in six days God created heaven and earth. A seven, that on the seventh day he rested from all he had made. An eight, of the eight righteous persons preserved from the deluge; namely, Noah and his wife, with his three sons and their wives. A nine, of the nine lepers cleansed by our Saviour. There were ten, but only one returned to offer his tribute of thanks. And a ten, of the ten commandments that God gave Moses on Mount Sinai, on the two tables of stone." He took the Knave and put it aside. "When I see the Queen it reminds me of the Queen of Sheba, who came forth from the farthermost parts of the world to hear the wisdom of Solomon, for she was as wise a woman as he was a man, for she brought fifty boys and fifty girls, all clothed in girls' apparel, to stand before King Solomon, for him to test which were boys and which were girls; but he could not until he called for water to wash themselves. The girls washed up to their elbows, and the boys only up to the wrists of their hands; so King Solomon told by that. And when I see the King it puts me in mind of the great King of heaven and earth, which is God Almighty; and likewise his Majesty King George the Fourth, to pray for him."

"Well," said the mayor, "you have given a good description of all the cards save one, which is lacking."

"Which is that?" said the soldier.

"The Knave," said the mayor.

"If your Honour will not be angry with me," returned Richard, "I can give you the same satisfaction on that as on any in the pack."

"No," said the mayor.

"Well," returned the soldier, "the greatest Knave I know is the serjeant who brought me before you."

"I don't know," said the mayor, "whether he

be the greatest Knave or no, but I am sure he is the greatest fool."

The soldier then continued: "When I count the number of dots in a pack of cards, there are three-hundred and sixty-five, — as many days as there are in the year. When I count how many cards there are in a pack, I find there are fifty-two, — so many weeks are there in a year. When I reckon how many tricks are won by a pack, I find there are thirteen, — so many months are there in a year. So that this pack of cards is both Bible, Almanack, and Prayer-Book to me."

The mayor called his servants, ordered them to entertain the soldier well, gave him a piece of money, and said he was the cleverest fellow he ever heard in his life.

There are several variations of this story, one being written in the French language and in rhyme; but as their theme is nearly identical with the one quoted, it is unnecessary to repeat them.

It is supposed that the visiting-card now in common use derived its origin from a custom, quoted by Mr. Taylor, of writing messages on the backs of playing-cards, — a practice which is mentioned in the "Spiritual Quixote," a novel of George the Third's time. This practice is also mentioned in "Henry Esmond," where an invitation is sent on a ten of Diamonds; and it was not confined to the novelist's world, as it was evidently the custom in America before the Revolution, for some of these invitations still exist and are treasured among family relics. There is one belonging to an American family which bears an invitation from Sir Jeffrey Amherst, printed on the back of the King of Clubs, to one of the fair damsels of his day; and this was dated 1769. Another card which apparently belonged to the same pack bore on its back an invitation to dinner from the same General to Mr. Ten Eyck for this same anniversary of Saint George's Day. It seems a strange coincidence that both these cards should have been sent to the author, — one of them coming from Boston; the other from Cazenovia, New York, where it was found in an old iron chest belonging to the Ten Eyck family. Another invitation card which is treasured in New York, carried an invitation from Miss Kitty and Miss Anna Livingston to Miss Laurence. These ladies are the ancestors of many well known townspeople, and the date of the invitation must have been about the same as that one issued by Sir Jeffrey Amherst, showing that it was a common practice during the middle of the last century to use playing-cards on which to write invitations.

Playing-cards have also been used to carry on their surface important messages; as before mentioned, the message written by the Duke of Cumberland was on a playing-card (the nine of Diamonds).

The fascination that games have for some people led to their being carried into queer places and strange company. The preacher's catastrophe and the soldier's apology have already been related; but cards have been played on the battlefield as well as by the home fireside, they have been used when travelling and even at the play, as one writer mentions that during a visit in Florence he was invited to join a game in an opera-box, where he was told that "good music added greatly to the pleasure of a whist-party, that it increased the joy of good fortune and soothed the affliction of the bad."

One writer has described a visit to a temple in Thibet, in which he found among other decorations "a couple of old playing-cards,"—the Knave of Hearts and the Ace of Acorns. Whether these were worshipped by the natives or considered as decorations, he could not discover.

The descendants of Lady Katherine Alexander, daughter of Major-Gen. Lord Sterling and wife of Col. William Duer, relate the following anecdote of her. The dame was fond of the rubber at Whist; and it is probable that in the beginning of the century cards were not as common nor as cheap as they are now, and that ladies carried their own packs with them to card-parties. At any rate, one morning while attending services at St. Paul's Church, New York, her Ladyship pulled her handkerchief out of her capacious pocket, and with it drew out a pack of cards, which, to the amusement of her neighbours and her own consternation, flew about the pew. Her mischievous sons never lost an opportunity of reminding her of the circumstance and teasing her about it.

PIPS, SUITS, AND COLOURS.

PIPS, SUITS, AND COLOURS.

THE emblems on the cards have been, since 1656, called *pips*, or *peeps*, and sometimes *points;* the former is the term generally used by card-makers and players, by which they designate the symbols at the present day.

The manufacturers call the court cards *têtes;* but this name has not been adopted among players. They are also frequently named *coat cards*,—a term which is supposed to be derived from the coats worn by the figures, in contradistinction to the other designs, which were sometimes flowers and animals as well as the symbols familiar to our eyes.

Many old and curious packs have survived the hard usage they were called upon to endure not only in the course of play, but also by their having been impressed into the book-binders' service, which has in many cases been the fortunate means of their being preserved to be prized and studied at the present day; and there are valuable collections in European museums which contain rare specimens of cards, not only delicately painted like the most beautiful miniatures on parchment and other materials, but also exquisitely engraved; and among them are some of the first specimens of that art.

The pack painted by Gringonneur, which has already been fully described, is in Paris; but this is a Tarot pack, which seems to have been the one in use at the French Court just before playing-cards in their modern dress were adopted. The cards prepared for the use of the French King, which were the first to be divided into suits and marked with the symbols of Hearts, Diamonds, Spades, and Clubs, are also preserved in the same place.

In the print-room of the British Museum is a portion of a pack which has the German marks of suits. These cards are stencilled and not printed or painted, and are supposed to date from 1440. They were discovered, as so many others have been, in the cover of an old book. There is another pack dated 1790, manufactured by Rowley & Co. "In it the Spade" (to quote from Mr.

Pips, Suits, and Colours. 193

Taylor) "is a kind of dagger, of a clumsy, inconvenient form. The Ace of Clubs is a cloverleaf in an oval. Diamonds clearly point to the original conventionalized form, being a veritable diamond, lozenge-shaped, with the facets of the cutting shown in relief. This idea of a quadrangular shape is involved in all the names of the Diamond suit, whether it be panes of glass or paving-tiles. Clubs," he declares, "has always been an anomaly."

The colours used in cards vary with the pips or the caprices of the card-makers. In the curious old pack mentioned by Mr. Singer, which dates from 1500 and perhaps earlier, there are only two colours used, and these were red and green; but they were not intended to mark the suits, they were used only on the costumes of the court-card figures. Some early Italian cards mentioned by Zani in his book entitled "Le Carte Parlante," were executed with a pale ink of a grayish tint, while others were printed with very black ink.

The Germans now call two of their suits *Roth* and *Grün*, or Red and Green, the emblems of which are a heart and a leaf.

There is still in existence a curious pack of

cards which were presented to Capt. D. Cromline Smith by a Brahmin of India in 1815, which is mentioned by Mr. Chatto. They were supposed to be a thousand years old. The Brahmin considered them to be a great curiosity, as they had been in his family from time immemorial. He did not know whether or not they were perfect, but believed that originally there were two more colours or suits. He said they were not the same as the modern cards, that none knew how to play with them, and that no books give any account of them. The pack consists of eight suits, each containing two honours and ten common cards. The backs are green, and they are painted in many different colours. Mr. Chatto remarks, that if they are even one hundred years old they must have been preserved with great care, and he is inclined to doubt their extreme antiquity.

The oldest set of French Piquet cards, known as the "Corsube pack," which were invented about 1425, or nearly five hundred years ago, are engraved on wood and coloured. The outlines are printed in pale ink, and the colours appear to have been applied by means of a stencil. A beautiful pack engraved on copper in the latter quarter of the fifteenth century was not intended to be coloured, as the symbols which marked the suits distinguished them without resorting to different hues.

Among other useful inventions, cards have been made for blind people, on the surface of which the pips were raised so as to be easily distinguished by aid of the fingers.

Within the past twenty-five years various alterations have been made in the cards. The court or face cards have been cut in halves, and so arranged that whatever end turns up in the hand the heads are always uppermost. The old figures showing the whole body are now only made for Faro (or Pharaoh) players. The custom of placing the numbers of the cards in their left-hand upper corner has lately crept in, having been demanded by Poker players, who glance rapidly at their hands and close them before betting on them. These cards are known to the card-makers as "Indexed," but are commonly called "Squeezers."

Although M. la Croix has declared that Étienne la Vignolles, sometimes called La Hire, who is supposed to have arranged the pack with the pips of Hearts, Clubs, Diamonds, and Spades, was inspired chiefly in his choice of these symbols by his heraldic knowledge and his military tastes, and that his Spades and Hearts were shields, and his Diamonds arrow-heads, it is worth noting that the Germans had chosen nearly identical devices to mark their suits, and that the Acorn is a Club, and Leaves and Hearts so closely resemble Spades and the French Cœur, that the similarity in form can hardly be due to a caprice of the card-maker or the fancies of a military man.

Cards have by many people been regarded for centuries with a superstitious awe, and accorded supernatural powers of divination; and it seems more probable that the devices were suggested by various symbols which were probably constantly before the eyes of men of the Middle Ages, particularly in churches or houses devoted to religious purposes.

Mr. Baring-Gould, in his "Curious Myths of the Middle Ages," mentions the discovery in 1850 of a Gallo-Roman palace near Pau in France. In one of the rooms the pavement consisted of squares which were ornamented with crosses of different shapes. Those of Saint Andrew "terminated in either a heart-shaped leaf or a trefoil." Here then may be seen the various devices adopted by the card-maker. On the "Carreaux," or diamond-shaped tiles, were displayed Clubs, Hearts, and Spades, beneath the feet of the worshipper in his church or the courtier in the palace; and to transfer the emblems to the card in place of the symbols used by the Oriental was an easy matter. The "Club," as we name it, is a favourite emblem of the Trinity, which has been used for centuries as its symbol; and we need not search for an Agnes Sorel or a Saint Patrick as the first to use the clover-leaf, and fancy that the French courtier meant to compliment the King's mistress by placing her device among the cards. It might just as well have been directly the reverse, and that she, seeing how pretty the leaf and how appropriate the pun on her name, might have adopted it from the card pips. It is quite possible that beside the Tarot cards there were others in use about the fifteenth century, and that their emblems became favourites in France and Germany, while Italy and Spain clung to those seen in the Saracen pack.

ODDS AND ENDS.

ODDS AND ENDS.

AMONG the other extravagant fashions of the French Court from the time of Charles the Sixth to that of Louis the Sixteenth, that of decorating the card-room, its furniture, accessories, and even the cards themselves, was by no means the least. It was perhaps fitting that the place in which enormous sums of money changed hands should be decorated as a shrine to the God of Play, and it is certain that they were luxuriously furnished and magnificently adorned. Under Louis the Fourteenth the cloths were of green velvet embroidered in gold and enriched with bullion fringes. The counters were of various metals, — mother of pearl, or other valuable substances. We read of a pack embroidered on white satin enriched with silver, and another one engraved on mother of pearl. Some of the more luxurious among the aristocracy ordered their cards from the most famous miniature painters of the day, in order to differ as widely as possible from the roughly produced and cheap cards used by the common people; and of course for these cards enormous prices were given. The decorations of the card-rooms were in harmony with the accessories of the tables, and tapestries were designed and woven to accord with the scenes which they surrounded; even within a few years one of the modern palaces in Europe has been adorned with mural decorations which represented the court cards of obsolete packs; and the four Knaves in picturesque costumes, life size and beautifully designed and executed, surround the card-room.

The tables were at first covered with green cloths which hung down and were held in place by their bullion fringes; but these covers were soon discarded, and the cloth was carefully pasted on the top of the table. Much ingenuity was expended in making the card-tables as handsome as were all the other details of the room. They were inlaid with beautiful woods, painted by celebrated artists, and richly ornamented in many other ways. They are nearly always square or partly rounded in shape, but are sometimes octagonal or three-cornered.

Mazarin seized on cards, which he was passionately fond of, as a means of instructing the young King Louis, and adopted the educational series, inducing the eight-year-old monarch to study history, geography, and other sciences by their means. This early introduction to cards led to their becoming the ruling passion of the life of that "Grand Monarch;" and under his reign the rage for cards reached a great height, and enormous sums were lost and gained. Mazarin was himself a notorious gambler; and his niece, although left an enormous fortune by her Cardinal uncle, died insolvent, the greater part of her money having been lost at cards. When Louis Quatorze reached the age of manhood, every evening from six until ten o'clock was passed in play. Even when engaged in necessary business, the game proceeded, the King deputing some of his courtiers to hold his cards during his absence. The knights of the green cloth being in such favour, a card-ball was proposed and given at Marley, Feb. 19, 1700, at which one dance was performed by the courtiers, who were dressed like the court cards of the pack. As Marley was the palace above all others in which gambling was carried to the highest extent, it was, says the historian, "the appropriate theatre for such an event."

The rage for playing cards was at one time as great in England as in France. James the First forbade cards in Scotland; but it was his favourite amusement. Charles the First did not disdain to create a monopoly of playing-cards by buying all those produced by the Card-makers' Company of London, and selling them out at a much higher price. Cards sold in 1545 for twopence a pack, and they must have been wretched specimens. The marriage of Charles to a French princess in 1629 may have introduced Piquet into England; it is mentioned in a book printed in 1649, at the same time with Cribbage.

The Roundheads professed to despise all frivolous amusements, and considered them sinful, although the early Christians evidently did not look on Dice and such games in the same light, as recent excavations in the Catacombs show that the graves there contained various implements of sport. "Dice-counters and gambling-boards," says a recent writer, "have been discovered in Christian tombs; and the boards, with their gay and inspiriting inscriptions ("Victus leva te; ludere nescis; da lusori locum," "Domine, frater hilaris semper ludere tabula"), do not differ at all from those with which the heathen had made merry. In the Domitilla Catacomb has been found the tomb of a master in the art of making Dice.

After the restoration of Charles the Second the court cards resumed their sway, and from that time to the accession of Queen Victoria, reigned supreme, from court circles down to the gypsies in their encampment in the fields. The rage for play reached such a pitch during the latter years of the reign of George the Third, that the Regent, his brothers, and his friends were all deeply involved in debt.

A story is related of the famous Dowager Electress of Saxony, who was devoted to the card-table and was not above taking advantage of her position and using it when opportunity offered. She one evening "committed some irregularity" (as cheating is termed when indulged in by a person of exalted rank), and excited suspicions of her honesty by her play. A courtier took notice of this, at which she expressed her surprise; thereupon he remarked, "Pardon, madame, my suspicions could not fall on you. *Sovereigns* cheat only for *crowns*."

Napoleon tried to while away the tedious hours of his captivity by playing cards. His favourite games were Vingt-et-un, Piquet, and Whist. The counters used for the last game were always of gold, and these have been carefully treasured by the descendants of his jailers. A nine of Hearts upon which he had written some English sentences is also preserved. It is related that he never entered on any enterprise or military operation without consulting a peculiar pack of cards, which were not provided with the customary marks of suits, and in fact were not divided into suits at all. These cards, which have been carefully preserved, were sent to the author for inspection. They were smaller than those generally used, and were printed in black on yellow pasteboard. Each card was surrounded with the signs of the Zodiac, and was divided by a black line drawn through its centre, and always contained two little pictures, one above and one below this line. Rings, Hearts, Roses, Cupids, Ladies, Kings, and Queens were displayed on these cards; but it was evident that they were not intended to be used for any game, and were only for purposes of divination. The cards were torn, and showed marks of age; and if not the pack originally used by the celebrated general, they may have resembled those he was said to have consulted and believed in.

THE END.

www.ingramcontent.com/pod-product-compliance
Lightning Source LLC
Chambersburg PA
CBHW032108220426
43664CB00008B/1176